BIGGER THAN LEADERSHIP:

STORIES OF INFLUENCE, INTENTION, AND INSPIRATION

BIGGER THAN LEADERSHIP:

STORIES OF INFLUENCE, INTENTION, AND INSPIRATION

Laura, thank you so much
for all of your support
with the book! I really
appreciate it, and I hope you
enjoy the book!
    Brittany Do

BRITTANY DO

NEW DEGREE PRESS

BIGGER THAN LEADERSHIP
Stories of Influence, Intention, and Inspiration

ISBN   978-1-63676-735-2 *Paperback*
           978-1-63730-032-9 *Kindle Ebook*
           978-1-63730-134-0 *Ebook*

Table of Contents

Introduction   9

PART 1:   All About Leadership   17
Chapter 1: Leadership   19
Chapter 2: Act on Your H.E.A.R.T.   31
Chapter 3: Catch the Leadership Bug   41

PART 2:   Be Intentional   53
Chapter 4: Intentionality   55
Chapter 5: Better Together   67
Chapter 6: Inspire Confidence   79
Chapter 7: Strength Redefined   91
Chapter 8: Failing Is Good   105
Chapter 9: Work with Others, for Others   117
Chapter 10: Listen with Your Heart   129

PART 3:   Inspire Your Life   139
Chapter 11: Live Your Life Purposefully   141
Chapter 12: It's the Little Things   153
Chapter 13: Learn How to Juggle   161
Chapter 14: Lead Yourself   173
Chapter 15: Reminders   185

Resources   191
Acknowledgments   195
Appendix   199

For those who are simply trying to human together, and for those who are sharing their stories. Yes, that likely includes you, too.

Life is a book in the making, full of stories and people.

Introduction

If you bought a really nice but expensive shirt for $200, what would you do with it? You could leave it in your closet to admire it, or maybe you'd decide to wear it every week to get the most bang for your buck. Perhaps you'd only wear it for special occasions—times when you know there's minimal chance of getting it dirty.

Now think about purchasing this same $200 shirt to simply spray paint over the design. Would you do it? What would it take to convince you? How easily do you think you'd be able to convince a friend to spray paint one of their own shirts? Not just any shirt, but the same one that's worth $200. Would you be able to do it?

Esteban Gast, a comedian, entertainer, and friend of mine, told me a story from when he was in junior high school and was able to do just that. How, you might ask? Influence. Pure influence.

In junior high school, Esteban tried out for the basketball team. He remembered how during basketball tryouts, "everyone had these really expensive shoes. They were the Adidas Tracy McGradys. They're like $200 shoes. And

I had Kmart shoes." People trying out for the basketball team made fun of him, and he remembered them saying he wasn't going to make the team without the Tracy McGradys, although he knew if he wasn't going to make the team, it'd be because he was bad at basketball.

Although Esteban was frustrated, he noticed how the Tracy McGrady shoes were really colorful. Deciding he was going to spray paint his Kmart shoes and wear them to school, he "remember[ed] thinking, 'I need to make this look cool.'" His confidence in wearing the spray-painted shoes worked; other kids thought what he did was cool, so a few other people spray-painted their own shoes. This was when something clicked. Esteban noticed that "what's cool is made up...They're not real rules. I can say 'this is cool,' and people did it...I remember guys spray painting their $200 shoes to match my twelve-dollar ones."

Esteban didn't think people followed his lead in spray painting his shoes because he was considered "cool," but rather because he had inadvertent influence on them. He realized leadership involves contagious emotions. For example, if a teacher were angry in the classroom, the classroom would feel weird. On the flip side, if the teacher were having a really good day, students would also have a really good day. Even if the teacher didn't explicitly say they were having a good day and simply started class with a smile, the students would feel a sense of calm.

Esteban has influence. I have influence. You have influence. Now, the next step is figuring out what we do with it.

People often silo leadership into parts of their lives. They only think of how they are leaders at school, work, or at home, but usually not all three simultaneously. Leadership is seen in all aspects of life; if we don't see how, we just need to look a little harder. Once we are aware of how to redefine leadership, this is when things shift.

There is a general distrust of people who call themselves "leaders." Why? Because some leaders focus on the wrong aspects of what it means to be a leader. With the words "leader" and "leadership," there comes a certain connotation, and one I believe is caused by confusing leadership with management. People think leadership revolves around having a high title and requires the power to tell people what to do and how to do it. There can be a lot of yelling and negative emotions involved in this. These people believe normal, everyday people, like them, can't and aren't leaders, and that there is only one style or type of effective leadership. The path to leadership is a difficult one, and others believe it's too late for them to be a leader.

Thankfully, this is not the case at all—leadership is inclusive. Everyone is and can be a leader. Although there are countless definitions about leadership showcasing what leaders do, I believe it's about influence, intention, and inspiration. Examples of leaders include the people I mention in this book...and also you. It's often the unforeseen leaders serving others with the best stories.

What is leadership about? What are influence, intentionality, and inspiration about? How do these appear in your life, not just once in a blue moon, but every day? Basically, why should I care about reading this book?

Even if you don't realize it, you are a leader. Are there people you interact with? Yes. Do you have some level of influence on these people? Yes. Congratulations—you're a leader, and you always have been.

Leadership is a constant journey and one that is laborious, but it's never too late to start. In fact, you are probably leading in ways you didn't realize. Managers do have their title and power, but leaders simply do not need one. They inspire others around them to see their vision and take action while managers impose their vision onto others without worrying if they also see their vision.

Each person's journey looks different. It starts during different times, at different places, and with different people. No matter what, it's essential to understand how to develop your influence in a way that's authentic to you.

I wanted to write about leadership because it's something I've had the privilege and luck to learn more about at a rather young age. I was in junior high when I decided to run for an official leadership position, and I've been hooked ever since. Many of my leadership experiences have helped shape the person I am today; I do believe they have shifted my perspective and truly see and realize the impact I have on others.

In the first two weeks of my sophomore year in high school, I got pulled aside by the Associated Student Body (ASB) president. We just had elections to determine the sophomore class positions. I had applied to be class treasurer because I'd always liked working with numbers; they just made sense to me. There were also multiple people running for the president and vice president positions, and by running for treasurer, I'd be unopposed. I didn't want to be the president or vice president, and frankly, I didn't have enough self-confidence to run against everyone.

When I got stopped on my way to class, I was a little confused and worried I had done something wrong. The "Hey, could I talk to you?" led to us sitting down on a nearby bench outside and him breaking the news to me—the ASB executive board officers, the people who were choosing the sophomore class officers, didn't think I would be a good fit for the position of treasurer.

This was pretty devastating to me, especially since I knew I had run unopposed. He said he couldn't tell me who had gotten the role of treasurer but wanted to talk to me about it. Then, he said another surprising thing; the executive board had decided that I'd be the best fit for class president. He gave me a piece of paper where he had written down, "Don't act through power, act through influence," as he reminded me that influence is more powerful than power itself.

***

John C. Maxwell talks about the Law of Influence in his book *The 21 Irrefutable Laws of Leadership* and how "The true measure of leadership is influence — nothing more, nothing less." I agree how influence helps cultivate leadership, but I believe there are other elements in this equation that help establish this influence.[1]

From communication to trust, vulnerability to empathy, and confidence to inspiration, there are so many more elements tied to leadership that go beyond the preconceived notion of what it means to be a leader.

---

1   John C. Maxwell, *The 21 Irrefutable Laws of Leadership: Follow Them and People Will Follow You* (Nashville: HarperCollins Leadership, 1998), Page 24.

I've been lucky enough to be able to talk with a wide range of people, from current high schoolers to retirees. I interviewed eighty-five people, and this includes students, business professionals, podcast hosts, entrepreneurs, fellow authors, teachers, speakers, and many more.

In his TEDx Talk, Peter Anderton sums it up nicely when he says, "Every single one of us can make a difference. Every single one of us is a leader in some way or another because leadership isn't actually about position. Leadership is about who you are."[2] People can and do change during their leadership journey and life journey. You just need to be receptive and willing to try things that will push you out of your comfort zone.

I believe that leadership is founded on *influence*, and with *intention*, you can *inspire* others around you. These three I's are prevalent in not only leadership, but life overall.

Leadership is a timeless and ageless skill and one you can constantly improve. Regardless of whether or not you've gained the experiences needed to understand influence, intention, and inspiration, countless lessons from the stories within this book are beneficial to all. I'd highly recommend this to anyone who loves listening to meaningful stories and believes genuine human connection is one of the best gifts in the world.

Even if you don't feel like you're ready to dive into this journey headfirst, remember that's okay because you have the support of the people around you, the knowledge from all these stories, and pure determination.

Since this book is focused on leadership and how and why it connects to life, there are related topics emphasized in

---

2   *TEDx Talks*, "Great leadership comes down to only two rules | Peter Anderton | TEDxDerby," July 25, 2016, video, 17:29.

this book, such as intentionality, mentorship, connection, balance, empathy, confidence, communication, inspiration, purpose, and failure.

I wanted to incorporate as many stories as possible in my book; I believe that stories are engaging and interactive, which lead to a better way of not just learning something, but truly understanding it. I love being rapt in stories myself, so I wanted this to be my own way of influencing others, through the stories that have influenced me. Stories are also more memorable, and FMRI (functional magnetic resonance imaging) studies show that storytelling lights up more regions of the brain than straight facts.[3]

Together, we will dive deeper into stories about:

- An inspiring blind woman completing a triathlon

- A traveling company that helps kids learn English through musicals and performances

- How powerful the words "I think you'd be good at it" are

- The reason for intentionally meeting people from various countries and how this pertains to leadership

- Near-death experiences and how they serve as a powerful reminder of how short life is

So, what are you waiting for? This journey isn't going to start by itself, especially since it's your own unique leadership journey. There's no time like the present, so let's get started. This will be quite the adventure—please hop on board and make yourself *uncomfortable* because that's the best way to learn and grow.

---

3   "Why Storytelling Works: The Science," *Ariel Group* (blog), December 26, 2020.

PART 1:

ALL ABOUT LEADERSHIP

Chapter 1: Leadership

———

"Life is a journey and sometimes we go around in circles."
—*Peter Anderton*[4]

Can you tell me about your leadership journey? In every interview I've done for this book, this is the question I chose to start with. Although this is a fairly simple and straightforward question, the stories I've heard are usually anything but; that's what makes each person's journey inimitable. The fascinating thing about life (and thus leadership) is that it doesn't matter where or when your journey begins.

When navigating this wild journey called life, it's so full of roots and trees that you end up lost in the forest without realizing. You don't know where you're headed or how to get there, but that's perfectly alright. If you were on a long hike, too focused on which turn to take, at which moment, and how long you've been walking for, then you'd miss seeing the beautiful simplicity of nature in front of you.

---

4   *TEDx Talks*, "Great leadership comes down to only two rules | Peter Anderton | TEDxDerby," July 25, 2016, video, 17:29.

By focusing too much on the beginning and the end, you miss the best part (hint: the journey itself).

Leadership is Complicated

It was a normal Friday evening, and I was interviewing a fellow college student Beth about her experiences in leadership. Beth was telling me about a difficult time where she had to navigate a sensitive issue with a group of other students. She wasn't feeling confident in how she handled the situation, but she was glad she had addressed the issue rather than left it alone.

As she told me her situation and how she reacted, I thought of an analogy—one that I repeated to her. If you're trying to housebreak a dog and it ends up going to the bathroom on your new, lovely carpet, would you clean it up right away or leave it there? If you act immediately, you have a higher chance of erasing any traces of it; it will also decrease the chance of your dog going to the bathroom in the same spot again. However, if you just leave it there or ignore it by throwing a blanket over to hide it, the smell will linger and get worse. What you ultimately do is your decision, but it is important to recognize and understand the consequences.

Leaders face difficult situations—you'll have to make some tough decisions, but this is almost expected. Step one is taking action despite fear or hesitation in these situations. Without change, progress is impossible.

We are the culmination of our experiences, good and bad. Everyone has their own unique story to tell, and you can't know and understand every single tiny detail and facet of someone's life. Life is a beautifully complicated thing, and so is leadership.

Definition

If you ask five people what their definition of leadership is, you'll get five different answers—everyone has their own unique definition.
Through interviewing over eighty-five people about their respective leadership journeys, I've heard numerous definitions of leadership. Here are five that stood out to me:

- "I think when you take your ego out of it and serve a group greater than yourself, going beyond yourself, to me, that's true leadership." —Caitlin Logue

- "Ultimately, I think [leadership] boils down to two things. One is connecting with other people, and two is surfacing something within them that they may not see within themselves." —Andrew Riis

- "There's no cookie cutter right answer of how to do [leadership]. And everyone inherently has influence and inherently is a leader." —Rayna LaFave-Clark

- "I would say [a leader] is someone who inspires another to take action, and it requires intention. But the ultimate kind of leadership is servant leadership. It's about taking the ego out of the equation and putting another's highest good in its place, which is a never-ending battle; it's not easy. But what makes it easier is to have the humility to admit we don't have all the answers." —Madeline Steitz

- A leader is "being someone who can influence others to the extent that people change their behavior or...

influencing a situation to the extent that it changes, whether it's individual behavior or social structure and improving it or anything in between that spectrum." — Ben Fields

- "I honestly think [leadership] is being able to find opportunities that make people say 'oh my god, I thought I was the only one'...that's a really powerful leadership act, to give people permission to not feel alone." —Drew Dudley

There's no singular definition of leadership because there are so many facets of it like humility, service, connection, inspiration, influence, intentionality, impact, and countless others. This is why leadership is in the basic essence of life.

Of course, there are certain categories and types of leadership, like transactional leadership, transformational leadership, autocratic leadership, servant leadership, charismatic leadership, and democratic leadership.[5] I wanted to focus on something different, though. Something like life and leadership.

Life and leadership are connected more than you may initially think. Although leadership has been around for far longer than it has been studied, there's still so much to learn about it. The concept of leadership began in the 1700s, but scientific research regarding it started in the 1900s.[6]

---

5   Kat Boogaard, "What Kind of Leader Are You? 8 Common Leadership Styles (and Their Pros and Cons)," *Getting Ahead, The Muse*, accessed March 1, 2021.

6   Albert S. King, "Evolution of Leadership Theory," *SAGE Publications* 15, no. 2 (April 1990): 43-56.

"Leadership is one of the most observed and least understood phenomena on earth." —James MacGregor Burns[7]

The more we begin to understand how much there is to leadership other than confusing it with management, siloing it into one part of our life rather than accepting that it is in all aspects and areas, and believing we are not leaders due to a lack of title and power, the more aware we are of it, especially in unexpected situations.

One way—and certainly not the only way—that I have defined leadership is through influence, intention, and inspiration. I've looked for these three elements in the people I know and stories I've heard when deciding which of the many I should include in this book.

The Beginning

Is there one story you've heard so many times before that you feel like you could recite it yourself? Maybe this is a family story or one in a book or video that you've read or watched countless times. For me, an example of this is actually John Norlin's story. It was senior year, and John was the Associated Student Body (ASB) President at his high school; his ASB advisor Brent Grothe told him the other students were counting on him and asked him what he was going to do as president. I've grown so used to hearing this story a certain way and knowing John in this setting that I expected him to retell this story to me in our interview when I asked him how his leadership journey began.

However, when I was actually talking with John, now the co-founder of CharacterStrong, a company that focuses

---

7   Ibid.

on teaching character development to teachers and students alike through social-emotional learning curriculum, he didn't tell me that story. John told me how he started playing hockey at a young age and how he even went to hockey school at the University of British Columbia every summer. Here, they emphasized, "It's who you are as a person, it's your character, how we treat people, how you are while playing the sport." In these moments, John realized when he was playing hockey, he wasn't always being kind to others because of his competitiveness. At the hockey school, one thing they wanted the students to learn was getting into the habit of asking how they can help. This simple concept was emphasized, and John liked who he was in those moments more than when he was a "competitive jerk who [was] all about winning."

Everyone's leadership journey starts somewhere and in their own way. Even if you're familiar with someone's story, they might surprise you.

Similarly to how John's leadership story began, when Daphne D'sa, a current college student at the University of Washington, started competing in the Future Business Leaders of America (FBLA) as a freshman in high school, all she knew was that she wanted to get involved immediately. It wasn't until the second FBLA competition, the State Business Leadership Conference, when Daphne realized that FBLA "was this opportunity for students to really bond and get to know each other and be supportive of each other." This was really encouraging for her because she hadn't previously seen students support each other like she did in FBLA.

This led to Daphne joining another club similar to FBLA—this time in her sophomore year. She chose DECA, a student organization for high schoolers to compete in business-related events. There was an upperclassman in DECA who was Daphne's unofficial mentor and took her under her wing. She "was super encouraging and super supportive" since the beginning of the competition timeframe. Unbeknownst to Daphne, her mentor had placed first at the International Career Development Conference (the highest level of competition in DECA) the year before. This year, they were competing in the same category, but her mentor still made sure to wish Daphne good luck and that she was feeling secure and excited at each level of competition. Through these actions, "she showed me that I wanted to be a mentor for somebody else, like she had been for me," which is why Daphne ran to be FBLA co-president going into her junior year of high school.

Daphne's unofficial mentor embodied influence, intentionality, and inspiration. She personally influenced Daphne through being intentional with her time and words of affirmation, thus inspiring her to pass it forward and be a mentor for someone else.

"Be somebody who makes everybody feel like a somebody."
—Anthony J. James

People inherently have value. That's right; *you* have value. One thing that makes leaders special is their skill in helping people realize how much value they have, especially the people who don't already realize this.

There's no one-size-fits-all kind of leader or style of leadership because of how different everyone is. Leaders do inspire and directly influence others, but this influence looks different.

Influence is the culmination of time, energy, and intentionality that you put in to develop something beautiful. Take Robert Downey Jr., one of Hollywood's highest paid actors, for instance. He has spent most of his life acting in movies and has had a huge influence on Abi Chandru, a college student at the University of Washington, because of his grit and perseverance.

Robert Downey Jr. didn't have a typical upbringing. He was introduced to marijuana by his father at eight years old, and this turned into a way of bonding with his father. This early exposure to marijuana led to substance abuse issues later in his life. What inspires Abi about Robert Downey Jr.'s story is that throughout his highest highs but especially his lowest lows, he "never gave up. He kept pushing and trying to learn from his past mistakes, which sometimes went well, sometimes didn't go well." How he was able to persevere through all the challenges in his life and become the very well-known Iron Man inspires Abi to not give up regardless of whatever obstacles he encounters in his own life. Abi knows that in the end, everything will work itself out, and he will be alright.[8]

Despite his atypical upbringing and early use of cannabis, Robert Downey Jr. went on to positively influence countless individuals and inspire them to keep pushing through and persevere through their own challenges.

What Kind of Leader Should I Be?

I'll be touching on various aspects of life strongly related to what being a good leader is about. Things like

8   "Robert Downey Jr's Heroic Recovery: From Addict To Iron Man." DreamLife News (blog), June 26, 2020.

community, failure, mentorship, involvement, vulnerability, consistency, humility, kindness, balance, trust, empathy, communication, discomfort, inspiration, confidence, selflessness, passion, and more.

I know you probably read the paragraph above and thought to yourself "Wow, that's...quite a lot of different topics. Are you sure leadership involves everything?" Don't worry, I'm just getting started.

Again, there is no one kind of "leader" because everyone leads differently. There are certain people who prefer working closely with people and really diving into that sense of community while others prefer getting things crossed off the to-do list. That's completely okay because no one is wired the same—frankly, both are equally important. Without relationship-oriented people, it can be more difficult to work with a group of people during stressful times. Without task-oriented people, it can be harder to manage approaching deadlines. It's really all about finding a balance that works best for the team.

Someone who realized this pretty quickly is Jack Hanscom, a college student at Willamette University. As a leader for the freshman orientation program to help transition incoming students into the Willamette culture and introduce them to the resources provided, he realized people have different strengths. While overseeing the program, which consisted of training about forty leaders, Jack noticed some leaders who were naturally more relational, more goal-oriented and goal-driven, and others who were a mix of both.

When working with his partner for their own group of fifteen freshman students and getting a feel for their

overall dynamic, Jack noticed how he's "super extro-
verted, super relational, and wired to be everybody's
friend...and [his] partner was very much like, 'I've memorized the schedule, I memorized all the duties, all the
tasks that we've done.'" Because of their complemen-
tary strengths, Jack and his partner worked really well
together—together, they had both the relational and task
components covered.

This really goes to show that people have different
strengths, and you can use this to your advantage. It's
not expected of anyone to be great at everything because
no one can guarantee that. However, you can determine
what your strengths are, so it's easier to create a team of
people with complementing strengths, which makes the
team more balanced. This doesn't mean people shouldn't
work on developing their weaknesses, but it is helpful to
be aware of what you are and aren't good at. No matter
where you are in life, there is always room for improvement in anything, and not being good at something does
not equate to being a failure.

Everyone is a leader, and more importantly, everyone is
their own kind of leader. No two people are completely
the same, so how would two people lead the same way?
It wouldn't be reasonable to expect yourself to be the
same leader as a public figure, a role model, or even the
person you know best.

One Thing

Instead of trying to be someone you're not, just focus on
one thing: "Leave people better than you found them,
especially those with the least amount of power." This is

the leadership principle that has resonated the most with Esteban Gast, previously mentioned in the introduction, throughout his own leadership journey. Whenever Esteban feels like he is not being as intentional or thoughtful as he could be, he reminds himself of the leadership principles that he lives by. Doing this allows him to realign his actions and values, thus reenergizing himself; he is focusing on the balance between giving to and serving others as well as self-care and self-love. Esteban looks inward and asks, "Who am I, and how do I want to contribute to the world?"

This principle is a great rule of thumb because it's such a simple concept to incorporate into our own lives. Three easy things you could do every day is hold the door open for the people walking behind you, smile at those around you, and say "Have a great rest of your day" to people you converse with before parting ways. These small things can go a long way and are just as valuable and meaningful as the large, grand gestures.

When we encounter people who are having a rough day or week, what do we usually suggest to them? I know that I often find myself telling others to take a break and get some rest. But when we're at work or in another professional environment, how often does this actually happen? Coonoor Behal, the founder and CEO of Mindhatch, found herself in this situation when her assistant was having a tough week. Instead of brushing it off, Coonoor told her, "Hey, take the rest of the week off."

Her assistant declined, but Coonoor insisted, saying that "whatever we had planned for this week, it can wait." When her assistant was still hesitant because she needed the money, Coonoor clarified and said "When I said take the week off, I meant paid time. Still invoice me for the regular amount of hours."

Coonoor certainly left her assistant better than she found her through seeing and meeting her need. She says these are the moments where leaders can choose to be human and not just do things by the book. If something can wait a few days, then it would be worth considering meeting the needs of the people who are around you rather than meeting your personal wants.

This is part of what being a leader entails: Sacrificing something ideal in the short-term for something better in the long-term. Since Coonoor understood and prioritized her assistant's needs, this strengthened the personal bond between them. Her assistant realized that Coonoor truly cared more about her health and well-being than checking something off the to-do list. Choosing to understand and act on your principles is important, especially when it affects others around you. Empathy is the key here—understanding how someone feels and why will make it easier for you to make a decision best for everyone.

Welcome to the world of influence, intention, and inspiration. Leadership is incredibly unique to each individual, but we're happy to have you here. I hope you're as excited as we are for the rest of your journey. The real question is what's next? What are you going to do now that you understand how you (and everyone else) have influence, thus qualifying you a leader?

Chapter 2:
Act on Your H.E.A.R.T.

If not you, who?

If not now, when?

"If you spend the rest of your career leading with love as the top priority, you will look back one day and realize that you made a significant, positive impact on the people around you and that you empowered them to make a positive impact on many others...this is probably the only measure of success that truly matters." —Matt Tenney[9]

The heart is one of the most important parts of the human body. Considered a vital organ, it pumps blood to the rest of our bodies and ensures there is sufficient oxygen and nutrients throughout. As humans, we cannot physically live without a heart because it's what enables our bodies

---

9   *TEDx Talks*, "Why the Best Leaders Make Love the Top Priority | Matt Tenney | TedxWestchester," December 5, 2019, video, 9:52.

to function properly. Connecting to the quote above, love is a needed element in leadership. It is part of what enables empathy and understanding others, and it parallels the heart we rely on so much as humans. We need the heart and love to keep us going in life and in leadership.

To live fulfilling lives, we need to figure out what drives and motivates us. Sounds pretty simple, right? The catch is that our passions differ and can change over time. When we face difficult situations, it's easy to react out of feelings, which makes it a bit more difficult to figure out how to best lead and live. Just like how we depend on our hearts, we can use love to keep our passion for leadership alive and strong.

Effective Leaders Lead with H.E.A.R.T.

Acronyms are always useful for remembering a concept. One company that focuses on personal and professional development, Rise Up For You, teaches kids that effective leaders lead with H.E.A.R.T. This is an acronym Dakota Rader, the director of programs and development at Rise Up For You, shared with me, and it lists certain characteristics of effective leaders.

Leaders are:

- Hands-on

- Emotionally intelligent

- Accountable and hold others accountable

- Relatable

- Transformational

Hands-on

What being a hands-on leader looks like is getting involved and making decisions in tough situations.

While she was helping manage a peaceful Black Lives Matter protest that she was speaking at, Christy Kioko was put in one of these situations. When she and the rest of the protesters were taking a knee for George Floyd, they encountered an All Lives Matter group who came and anti-protested. The two groups began to get rowdy, and Christy and the other speakers knew they needed to de-escalate immediately before things became violent. Christy wanted to keep her word that it would be a peaceful protest. She and the other speakers led everyone away from the other group, "and hundreds of people followed [their] lead, but then there was a very small group of people that stood back and actually got really upset with [her]" because they thought Christy was giving up and letting the other group win.

As a hands-on leader, you're expected to make hard decisions and take action. You can't always lead from the back and simply watch things unfold.

There always will be people who don't always agree with your decision, and "you take the heat" like Christy did, but you have to be okay with that. Christy realized, "You have to be confident in what you're doing and believe that you made the right choice. If you're reacting on your gut feeling, almost 90 percent of the time, your gut feeling's the right way to go." It's never a pleasant experience to have to take the lead and make certain decisions other people might not want to, but it is one of the things that comes with leading others. In the end, Christy made the decision she believed was best for everyone; she took action rather than sitting back and leaving the situation to chance. As a leader, this is especially when working with a large group of people. You need to take a stance and stand by it.

Emotionally Intelligent

Another trait of effective leaders is having emotional intelligence (EQ). There are four main categories of EQ: self-awareness, self-management, social awareness, and relationship management.[10]

"She was very hurt and therefore angry at the world." Rayna LaFave-Clark, a nursing student at Pacific Lutheran University, was a mentor to a middle schooler who was having some trouble in school. As her mentor, Rayna was supposed to help with her homework. However, Rayna "threw that out the window because that's not what this girl needed in [her] opinion. She didn't need help with homework; she needed somebody to listen to her and to be with her." After two years of consistently supporting her mentee and simply creating a space for her to voice her frustrations, her mentee brought her grades up and was making all As and Bs in school. Rayna noticed a bigger change than just in her grades. Over these two years, Rayna has taught her kindness and leadership lessons, including what she had learned at Mt. Adams, a leadership camp, as a delegate. She realized her mentee has

---

10   Daniel Goleman and Richard E. Boyatzis, "Emotional Intelligence Has 12 Elements. Which Do You Need to Work On?" *Harvard Business Review*, February 6, 2017.

completely transformed, and "every week asks if we can write words of affirmation notes to people."

"Everyone wants to be supported and heard and loved." — Rayna LaFave-Clark

If Rayna had simply tutored her mentee in the academic sense, then maybe her grades would have improved the same amount, but by being willing to listen, this allowed for more change than in just grades. She made sure her mentee felt heard and supported. Rayna exhibited empathy (social awareness) and coached her mentee (relationship management) because she recognized how at the time, this was more important and critical than only helping her academically.

Accountable

Effective leaders hold themselves and others accountable. They need to commit to following through with what they said they would accomplish. There are exceptions especially when emergencies come up, but keeping up with the smaller deadlines for long-term projects always helps mitigate stress overall. Accountability certainly goes beyond simply working with others in group projects because you're expecting the best from yourself and the people you're working with.

For Simrah Shaik, when she was rushing her professional business fraternity, she held a leadership position as the president of her cohort. One thing she held herself accountable for during that semester of the rushing process was holding her own cohort accountable—all rushees needed to wear a specific pin every day, otherwise they would get penalized. Simrah had a routine where "every morning at six, I would wake up, and I would message in the group chat 'Hey guys, don't forget to wear your pin.'" This reminder kept Simrah accountable for serving the other rushees as president and also kept everyone else accountable for remembering to wear their pins. By taking a few seconds out of her day to be intentional, Simrah helped the other students in her cohort. This underscores how serving others by keeping everyone accountable does not need to be for something major. Effort means a lot no matter how large or small the task at hand is.

Relatable

Genuine human connection stems from being able to relate to others. No matter what, we are more alike than we are different, and searching for this common ground between ourselves and others is a phenomenal and underrated tool. When you can relate to someone's story and really hear what they have to say, this action speaks much louder than any words you could utter. Even if you are unable to fully relate, intentionally trying to connect is better than putting in zero effort.

During the 2019–2020 school year, all students started school in person like normal but finished virtually. One English and leadership teacher, Sue Dunfield, missed the feeling of closure at the end since classes were all remote. Not liking the fact that usual in-person goodbyes would be given over a screen, Sue decided to write a postcard to every student she had that year. The byproduct of this decision "was ultimately taking a moment of gratitude and intentional thought about each individual person," as she told me in our interview, which helped reframe the overall negative situation. She recognized her decision to write a personal card to each student was one that would take time, which she did not have a lot of at the moment amidst grading assignments, but she wanted to make the time to do this for her students.

In her leadership class, there were some students who never participated virtually, but after she sent the cards to everyone, Sue received emails from them. One student shared how the past few months had been a difficult time for them. While it's easy for teachers to assume that kids are not engaging because they are checking out, it's better to give them the benefit of the doubt. By sending each of her students a letter, this level of personal outreach felt like a direct invitation to them to participate in return, which is why she believes she got these responses. Although Sue was missing out on her favorite part of being a teacher—the face-to-face interactions with her students—she made the most of the situation and showed her students that she cared about them.

When we're trying to relate to other people, what we can do is share something about ourselves so people can relate to us first, which establishes an initial connection. Being able to relate to someone is powerful, and it helps bring people together.

Transformational

Although we need to understand someone's story to relate to them, this is not needed to notice potential in others. Transformational leadership is all about vision and inspiring others to be the best version of themselves. It involves inspiration, motivation, and a bias for change.[11] Leaders are able to see the potential in not only themselves, but others as well. They seek out people who have certain strengths and help them create opportunities to cultivate these strengths so they can reach their potential.

Victoria Brodsky, entrepreneur and founder of DrinkLyte Co., went to a progressive K–8 school in California that emphasized group learning on a peer-to-peer level. This kick-started Victoria's leadership journey. Outside of academics, she focused on sports like volleyball, lacrosse, and cross country, and although she was never the best athlete, she was constantly an inspiration to her team members. One of the coaches noticed her efforts in going to every summer training session for the junior varsity volleyball team, and he gave her a leadership book to read.

This came as a surprise to Victoria because up until this point, "no one ever told me, 'Hey, we think you have really great leadership. We want you to read this book to understand it more and to be really self-aware of what we're seeing in you. And we want you to be the captain of the junior varsity volleyball team.'" Victoria liked inspiring others but didn't realize it had a name. After she read the book and learned about leading by example, she worked really hard to emulate this. One thing Victoria focused on was being early and ready to push harder than everybody else. Even though she wasn't the greatest at volleyball, she showed up, made sure everyone knew what

---

11   Sarah K. White, "What Is Transformational Leadership? A Model for Motivating Innovation," *CIO*, February 21, 2018.

they were doing and in the right mindset, and checked that people were happy.

Through leading by example, Victoria began her leadership journey via her coach who had demonstrated transformational leadership. He noticed how she exhibited certain traits, like showing up early and supporting her teammates, which suggested her raw potential in leadership, making him want to develop it by providing her with a book on leadership.

Transformational leadership involves creating opportunities for other people, especially when there are noticeable gaps. When Rutledge Long, the founder and director of Parachute Bridge, a non-profit that offers college students and young professionals a virtual career development program, finished graduate school, he had a vision. He was going to help reshape education through creating an experience that students could opt for. He believed that we "have to give students more real-world experiences and a better idea of who they are because they're working so hard to create a piece of paper to make someone else proud, then they figure out who they are and what they even want to accomplish." Rutledge wanted to flip this perspective because he knew how important it was for students to gain experiences where they struggle and endure hardships that will help shape and form them into leaders before college begins. This way, they are better prepared for the obstacles later on.

Rutledge is innovating what education means and looks like. This is a prime example of transformational leadership in action because he is actively changing the definition of education after realizing that there is potential to grow.

Ultimately, the only person you can control is yourself. You can choose what *you* and *only* you do. Thus, choose to lead with love and H.E.A.R.T. Trust the part of you that is itching to be a hands-on, emotionally intelligent, accountable, relatable, and transformational leader. Take action today rather than waiting for the perfect moment because there is no such thing. Don't wait, just do.

Chapter 3:
Catch the Leadership Bug

———

"When you figure out how to do life, you figure out how to do leadership." —David Robertson

My own journey in leadership started with me losing in an election.

Prior to running for treasurer in my sophomore year of high school, I ran for ASB Treasurer in the spring of my eighth-grade year at my junior high school for the following school year—I thought it was a good opportunity to get more involved at my school. Each candidate needed to recite their speech in front of the whole school, something I was terrified of doing; I was the person who loved to work behind the scenes and be as far away from the limelight as possible...and I also had stage fright. Despite this, I had spent hours drafting, refining, and practicing my speech in addition to putting flyers around the school. I wanted to shoot my shot, and I didn't want my efforts to go to waste.

When it was my turn to speak, I recall stepping up to the microphone. Time slowed down as I recited my speech, and all the noise around me disappeared. Although I made sure to look at the audience, I couldn't really see them—it was only me, the sheet of paper in my hand, and my pounding heartbeat. Before I knew it, I finished my speech and time, and my senses were back to normal. I was done, and I felt empowered because I had just faced one of my fears.

I later found out I had lost to another student, but it was still a great learning experience. The speech pushed me out of my comfort zone, and I discovered I was capable of speaking in front of over one thousand people. Thankfully I had gotten enough student votes to be offered another position, co-activities coordinator, which enabled me to begin exploring the world of leadership.

This was my first time in an official leadership role, and I was excited about it. When I spoke with Kyler Parris, someone I had known since the beginning of my leadership journey, he described my eighth-grade self as someone who was "quiet and shy, yet so enthusiastic to learn and help." At the time, I had no idea what I was jumping into; it was only my first steps in the continuous leadership journey I've been a part of since all those years ago.

Since then, I've been hooked on leadership—I suppose you could say that I caught the leadership bug, which I've decided has four core stages: fear, empowerment, exploration, and continuation. Even if you're scared of putting yourself out there and catching the leadership bug, sometimes you catch it anyway. Fear is tough to manage, but you can't let it stop you from doing something that you want to try, like leadership.

Fear

When Josh Holler, a senior audit assistant at Deloitte, started watching *Naruto*, a Japanese manga series and anime, he didn't realize how many life lessons he would take away from the show. One of these lessons is how "a lack of understanding is the definition of fear; you don't understand something, so you're afraid of it." This is demonstrated through the main character, Naruto Uzumaki; in the show, Naruto fights Pain, the leader of a large evil organization called Akatuski, who is trying to kill people but is as much of a metaphor as he is a character.

Rather than being so afraid of Pain and his determination to hurt others that he immediately kills him, Naruto decides to talk to him—he says, "I want to understand you; I want to understand...why you would do this sort of stuff," so they sit down and just have a conversation. Naruto takes the time to understand where Pain is coming from and why he tried to hurt others. Essentially, Pain's "whole philosophy was that everybody knows the same pain, everybody understands each other, and everybody's equal, and...if he makes the world feel the same pain, they'll all relate to each other and wars will stop."

To be able to truly impact others, "you have to understand [them] in order to get any kind of ground." Naruto was able to convince Pain that people could understand one another through love instead of violence and pain through their conversation—Pain trusted Naruto and let him try to change the world through love instead of pain. The metaphor in this moment of the show was that you don't fight pain with anger because it is better to seek to understand someone's anger.

I agreed with Josh and mentioned how this reminded me of my own fear of spiders. Since I didn't understand spiders, I was afraid of them. Fear can leave us stuck and uncertain, but we can remind ourselves to do our best to maintain a clear mind. When it comes to encountering spiders or other scary animals, it is easier said than done, but that's why it's so important to take the time to learn about what you're scared of to mitigate that fear.

If you are scared of something in your life but don't take the time to research it in hopes of a better understanding, this is synonymous to not being willing to listen to and have a conversation with it. I'm sure that if it were possible for me to communicate with spiders to better understand them, I wouldn't be as afraid of them. It's alright to be scared of doing something that makes you feel uncomfortable. As a leader, you just need to consider what you'll end up regretting more: trying something new, failing, and learning from that experience or not trying it at all.

Empowerment

Naruto had a huge impact on Pain and vice versa. You will often have the choice to hurt someone and make them feel embarrassed and inferior, or you can instead choose to make them feel capable, empowered, and inspired.

Someone who has had a profound impact on Jerico Agdan, a university student at Esade, is his mentor. While eating dinner one evening with his mentor, Jerico shared some goals he had and how his mentor responded was simple but left a lasting mark on Jerico. He told Jerico,

"Regardless of your situation, you are worth[y]...you are capable of achieving what you believe."

For Jerico, this was huge; he believed his mentor "was the gardener, and he helped me grow; he helped me flourish." Words do have an impact. Although something you say might not be a big deal to you, it can heavily impact another person—we truly do remember the way others make us feel, even when we don't recall what they specifically say. Since then, Jerico's entrepreneurial spirit has only been growing. He just needed that initial push of support and recognition of his potential, and he's been chasing after his dreams since then.

When you're looking back and reflecting on what your life has looked like up to this point, I'm willing to bet there have been some pivotal moments. Moments where you needed to make a critical but difficult decision. Am I going to stay up to finish working on this project but risk only getting three or four hours of sleep? There's this cool opportunity that I want to apply for, but can I manage everything on my plate plus one more? Should I stay after this event to talk to the speakers who I thought were really insightful or should I leave since the line is rather long?

When talking about pivotal moments in life with Caitlin Logue, the founder and CEO of 5280 Coffee Co., she brought up how she started her coffee company. She'd been on the fence about following her dream and love for coffee for some time because she wasn't sure what the future would entail. She told me "oftentimes, just validation for what you want[ed] to do [was] important—if you need[ed] someone to just say 'Hey, go for it'" because, although at the time she was working at another company and thinking about starting her own business, she was hesitant. While admitting this to someone who was established in the industry she was working in, they told her, "Why not? You have nothing to lose, you're still young. Go for it." This was the push she needed to officially change her dream of starting her coffee business into a reality.

One word or phrase you tell someone can be that slight boost of confidence they need to follow their dream and make it happen. How simple is it to just spend five or ten minutes talking with someone, really, *truly* hearing what's on their mind and what they have to say, and then support them? Incredibly simple, right? But how often do we take the time to actively listen to those around us without judgment and without being partially distracted by something else? Leadership is about influence, yes. But leadership and influence both involve listening with both ears, rather than just one.

In a world with so many distractions, this can be a difficult but incredibly worthwhile task. Everyone has something happening in their life at every given moment, yet you never know how much it will mean to someone else for you to take time to listen to them for even a few minutes.

As a leader, you have the ability to empower yourself *and* others around you, which results in catching the bug. Let's do it more often. You can empower yourself if you understand where and how in life you want to grow, though it can also look like finding a mentor who empowers you. Practicing active listening and being fully present with them is always worth your time and effort when empowering other people.

Exploration

You may be wondering how you catch the leadership bug amidst fear and empower yourself and others. First, take a moment to ask yourself some questions.

What are you most interested in? This can be more general, but try to think in specifics. Rather than saying traveling, maybe it's exploring new places and meeting people. Perhaps nature interests you, especially hiking because of the journey and beautiful views along the way.

Personally, I continued diving into other leadership experiences. I got more involved in clubs, and I began to realize how important leadership was, especially since you're learning and mitigating fear through your first-hand experiences. When you're able to get more involved with what you're interested in and passionate about, then it becomes even more enjoyable.

Sometimes you might be exploring your interests without even intentionally doing so. For David Robertson, founder of GrassFire Industries LLC and author on leadership, his own journey began a little different from my own. In college, he was required to take a couple leadership classes for the major he was in at the time, but then he "fell in love with leadership" and decided to pursue that instead. David ended up receiving not only his Bachelor's in Strategic Leadership but also his master's degree and is currently pursuing his doctorate in leadership. Now, through GrassFire Industries LLC, David teaches professional leadership and talent development training via a program for his clients. I think it's pretty safe to say his leadership journey has exceeded the length of the initial two college classes he needed to take back in college. Just trying new things can result in a new passion or hobby.

Another question to ask yourself is this: What are the values you hold close to your heart? Start off by finding a list of twenty or thirty values, then begin narrowing them down by the ones you prioritize the most to your top ten and then your top five values. (If you Google "list of values," there will be plenty to look through.) Values are always a great place to start because they often underlie our actions and beliefs.

One thing Minami Wakabayashi, a university student from Japan, prioritized when choosing which university to study at was the opportunity to study abroad. She valued meeting people all over the world, and this played a role in her ultimate decision to attend Waseda University, which has a variety of study abroad programs. Minami couldn't envision herself being at the same campus and mingling with the same people over her four years of university; this stemmed from having attended a high school in Singapore for her final two years before university where all her friends were international students who went to university in the United States.

Minami ended up pursuing a study abroad exchange at the University of Washington (UW), where she did get the opportunity to meet students from all over the world and found her place within different communities at and beyond UW. From different points in her life, she has friends in Taiwan, Singapore, Japan, the United States, and more.

Another trustworthy method for exploring your purpose is to write down a list of interests and hobbies you have. If you love animals, then volunteering at your local animal shelter is always a good option. I personally volunteered at my local shelter for nearly two years, and it is still one of my favorite experiences to date. I will warn you that you may feel the strong temptation to take one or all of the animals home with you, though.

Exploration is important for anything in life because how else would you know whether or not you enjoy doing something? It especially pertains to leadership because when you're seeking out new knowledge, you're automatically going to be a better leader because of it. We all have such diverse backgrounds and experiences, so when you're trying to be a leader who can relate to others, it's easier to have some knowledge to build off of.

Continuation

Just like when you're investing money in stocks, time in the stock market is better than timing the stock market—time in leadership is better than timing leadership. There is no "perfect" time to start being a leader, and once you begin, it's easier to continue doing so, especially when you have a purpose that drives you.

When Justin Nguyen, founder of *Declassified College*, started his podcast in 2017, he wouldn't have known he would gain over one hundred thousand followers within the span of a month on TikTok through creating short informative videos on how to win at college. He just had a vision, and a powerful one at that. Justin wanted to not just share essential cheat codes with college students through his podcast, like how to find scholarships and work on side projects, but also develop a more relevant and current platform for education. He understood that there were better ways to educate students outside of the classroom; he didn't wait for the so-called perfect moment or opportunity. He just went for it.

Justin believes that the reason why he had been so motivated to continue to work on *Declassified College* despite how it didn't generate much revenue initially is because "throughout my whole life I didn't have a why." In high school he loved playing soccer, but it wasn't his why. He was aiming to get a college scholarship and then perhaps play professionally, but this fell through when he broke his leg in his junior year of high school. Through his podcast, Justin has helped bridge the knowledge gap for college students by sharing what particular students have done to achieve their success, and this turned into his why.

When you believe in yourself and your why, and you continue to do the work, this is what matters the most in the end regardless of the number of people who believe in you. Justin continued his leadership journey because he determined what his why was and believed in it.

When Jonathan and Jerry founded Wonsulting in 2019, they didn't realize how many students' lives they would directly impact or how many people would soon be following their career advice in their many LinkedIn posts. All they had was a shared vision and mission. Their goal was to turn underdogs into winners, a goal inspired by their own past experiences facing obstacles as minorities trying to break into competitive fields at non-target schools.

Jonathan focuses on leading by example in his life and recognizes that through this, he's able to impact others more organically, especially through his stories on

LinkedIn. No matter what he is doing, Jonathan wants to "be able to have a huge impact on people...I just want to be remembered for who I am as a person." Through Wonsulting, Jonathan has helped bridge the gap between students at non-target colleges and their dream careers by providing recommendations on talking to professionals, building your professional brand, and finding people to connect with.

Jonathan and Jerry had their shared vision, and they didn't wait for a perfect moment to act. They just did it, and they shared their own personal stories along the way, which helped current university students relate to them. They became pioneers of their own and inspired thousands. Once their journeys began, they kept at it because they understood their driving purpose.

When you're looking for what makes you jump out of bed, ready and stoked to tackle the day, it takes time. It's always easier (and usually better) to start earlier rather than later, but remember everyone is on their own journey of catching their own bug—this doesn't mean you're automatically behind.

Ultimately, it's always great to seek out opportunities that both interest and excite you. Even if you're scared to try something new, empower yourself, explore, and continue trying anyway. Once you start getting involved after identifying your values, interests, and hobbies, oftentimes you'll find that you want to not only continue but deepen your involvement. The key is finding what you're passionate about, so it doesn't necessarily feel like work.

Just like how you're continually figuring out what life is all about, you're also figuring what leadership is about.

It truly is a long journey, and that's part of the beautiful process. This is the thing about leadership. It's not just something you can find at work or something you have to be born with. Different people need different things in their lives to be out of their comfort zones or empowered, but there's one similarity in the overall journey. Once you catch that bug, whether it's an entrepreneurial bug or a leadership bug, it's hard to stop looking at life differently. Figure out what the reason is behind what you do and find the people who will support, hear, and love you throughout your journey.

PART 2:
BE INTENTIONAL

Chapter 4:
Intentionality

———

"Leadership lesson #1: Names are important." —John Norlin,
co-founder of CharacterStrong

One of my favorite parts about leadership is the element
of intentionality. My name is Brittany, which originates
from the French peninsula. There are various ways to
spell it, so I've grown used to people misspelling my
name. This has made me be more intentional about paying attention to the spelling of other people's names.

I wanted to focus on the importance of being intentional
in leadership, particularly with names and relationships.

Hello My Name Is

According to *The Washington Post*, "A person's name is
the greatest connection to their own identity and indi-
viduality. Some might say it is the most important word
in the world to that person. It is the one way we can
easily get someone's attention. It is a sign of courtesy

and a way of recognizing them."[12] This is so important. People's names are inherently tied to their identity and who they are. By intentionally making the effort to ask someone how their name is spelled or pronounced, you are recognizing them as an important individual who matters because you're showing them you see them for who they are.

Jakub Zajíček, the co-founder and CMO of Speak On Podcasts, a podcast relations agency, who lives in the Czech Republic won't mind when people misspell or mispronounce his name. He's gotten his name misspelled and mispronounced so often that he has grown desensitized to it. His name is pronounced like "yah-koob" if you spelled it phonetically. Because I wanted to be intentional about pronouncing his name properly, I listened to it a few times on LinkedIn's name recording feature before interviewing him. Although Jakub is okay with people calling him Jacob ("jay-cub"), and he sometimes even goes by his initials, JZ, because it's faster and simpler, it's all up to personal preference. When you're making the effort to pronounce someone's name properly and correctly, you're showing them that you care and want them to feel heard and valued.

"We all just want to be seen, we want to be heard, and we want to be loved." —Devesh Tilokani[13]

In my first year of college at the University of Washington, I met one of my good friends, Ahlam Nur. For the first

12   Joyce E. A. Russell, "Career Coach: The Power of Using a Name," *The Washington Post*, January 12, 2014.

13   Devesh Tilokani, "Ep 097 - Is Listening More Important Than Talking?" November 4, 2020, in *Progressholic*, produced by Devesh Tilokani, podcast, 10:06.

few months of our friendship, I was hesitant and even scared to say Ahlam's name because it's a little harder to pronounce. It has a soft "ah" sound coupled with a brief pause before continuing to the second syllable; I didn't want to mess up and get the pronunciation wrong. We had been friends for so long, and I felt embarrassed that I wasn't confident in my ability to say my own friend's name. I kept telling myself that I was a terrible person and friend because I didn't already master the pronunciation of her name.

That's the thing about fear. It can hold us back and stifle us from doing what we actually want or intend to do, but eventually I stopped letting it hold me back. I wanted to pronounce her name correctly and even though I was scared, I did it anyway. Was it worth it? Absolutely. After I asked Ahlam to say her name and recited it back to her a couple times, it didn't even seem too difficult anymore. It's really just getting used to being intentional about asking people again and again, no matter how many tries it takes to get it right because *names do matter*. Most of the time when Ahlam introduces herself to people, they simply don't try saying it at all, or they even ask her if she has a nickname. Ahlam wishes more people would be willing to try to pronounce her name. She'd be "proud and happy that somebody gave it a shot."

"They want an easy way out on my name; they want to simplify my name…My name is still my name." —Ahlam Nur

Although it can be scary to ask someone how to properly pronounce their name, keep being intentional anyway. Don't let your inner thoughts withhold you from acting on your pure intentions. The more intentionally you live your life, the freer you'll feel because you will no longer be under the thumb of your emotions. Don't get me wrong, emotions are helpful, but not when you let them control the way you live your life.

There are also people with common names but perhaps not common spellings. Erinn Ford, executive vice president, advisor engagement with Advisor Group, has a common name, but her name is spelled with two N's. She emphasizes the importance of people's names in spelling and pronunciation because "to that person, their name spelled right, said right, is the most precious word in the language anybody can have." Whenever she sees the name Erin (one n instead of two), she immediately thinks, "Oh, that's not my name...by pronouncing it or spelling it right is the greatest form of honor because you're honoring [someone] as a unique individual."

Rather than assuming the way someone pronounces or spells their name, you can always ask. The worst that could happen is that your initial assumption is correct. Double checking means a lot to the person because it shows how you are being an intentional leader.

One person I spoke with—let's call her Sarah—had a memorable interaction with someone who we'll call Catherine. Sarah was emailing Catherine for an extracurricular activity she was involved in, and although Sarah currently goes by her given name, she had gone by a different name for professional reasons. Since Sarah decided to switch back to going by her given name, this is how she signs her emails, but she had both names listened on her LinkedIn profile just in case. While exchanging emails, Sarah noticed Catherine had addressed her by her past preferred name despite her obvious signature at the bottom of the emails. In a later email, Catherine even addressed Sarah by her last name. This irked Sarah because she was not being addressed by her preferred name even though she had purposefully included it in her email signature.

Everyone still makes mistakes regardless of our intentions. Mistakes remind us we are human, which is okay, but what matters is that we make an effort to recognize our mistakes, correct them, and internalize what we learned when moving forward. If you are uncertain about someone's preferred name, just ask them.

One day while working at my local YMCA, there was a girl who decided to draw a picture for me—a sweet gesture. I remember looking at the top of the sheet of paper. It said, "To Brittany," but behind the "-any", I could see a faint "-ney." I felt really touched; a young girl drew me a picture, addressed it to me, noticed I was wearing a name tag, realized she had misspelled my name, and corrected herself. It doesn't really matter that she misspelled it in the first place. What mattered more to me is that she recognized her mistake and fixed it immediately.

How often are we doing this in our lives? Is there a time you can think of where you were doing something wrong, realized it, and fixed it? Hopefully, yes. But could we all continue to be more cognizant of what we're doing and think of ways to do things more intentionally? Definitely—there truly is always room for improvement. Even when we're so used to going through the everyday motions of life, we can still look at things from a different angle. This will be a constant journey, and it's okay to be hesitant in asking others; intentionally make the effort anyway.

Touch a Heart Through Listening

Aside from the importance of intentionality in names, there are other areas in our lives where we can all be a little more intentional. This doesn't have to be a grand gesture—it can be something on a smaller scale. It's really the thought that counts.

One of the most impactful people for Ruth Huwe, a leadership professor at the University of Washington, was her mom. Her mom's intentionality touched her own heart through the small but meaningful things she would do. When Ruth was visiting home from college, she'd mention things to her mom in passing—one time, she mentioned how she really liked the garlic and pickles her mom had made her. Ruth's mom ended up making her "an entire quart of just the garlic. You don't think about how much work that is...just something to make your daughter happy." Intention goes a long way. When we live in the present and pay attention to what other people around us are saying, this creates endless opportunities to be more intentional in the way we act. It makes such a difference when someone who cares about you notes that you like a particular food and takes the time to prepare it as a gift.

When Houston Kraft, co-founder of CharacterStrong and author of *Deep Kindness*, and John Norlin were sitting down for dinner at the Cheesecake Factory, Houston noticed something John did that was minor but incredibly intentional. John was taking notes on their conversation so he could follow up with Houston in a couple of weeks. As his friend, mentor, and fellow co-founder of CharacterStrong, John is one of the most intentional people Houston knows, and "it's pretty fun to witness and watch him live the message so well."

I absolutely love this concept of purposely taking notes on a conversation with a friend so you can follow up with them at a later date. Even if you took notes right after the conversation, it would force you to pay more attention and focus on the person you're talking to. Just like anything, listening is a skill that can be improved upon with intention and practice.

As for the intentionality in friendship, Houston realizes some people take it for granted, but he understands how it truly is a gift—being able to still see John as intentional as ever a decade later is amazing. A simple "Hey, how has this thing you mentioned a couple weeks back been going?" can mean the world to someone because you're showing them that you were actively listening to them.

There are countless other small but meaningful things we can do as well. One of my favorite tools to stay organized is my large whiteboard calendar on my wall. After I forgot some important birthdays, I began writing them on my calendar. In addition, if I tell someone, "Hey, let's catch up again in a month or two," I'll actually add a reminder to my calendar as a note for myself to see what their availability looks like.

Sometimes the smallest things create the biggest impacts. Intentionality is simple, and these tiny actions build up. By being more intentional with what we do and how we do it, we are able to influence more people around us in a meaningful manner. Are you being intentional in the way that you serve them? Are you putting in the work despite realizing that effort is hard and tiring? Life is a journey full of experiences, both good and bad. When you live life more intentionally, there is more joy. This doesn't mean it becomes easy, but I do believe things get easier.

A quote by Dr. Martin Luther King Jr. is "Life's most important and urgent question is 'What are you doing for others?'" Serving others doesn't have to be huge or costly in any way—it just has to matter. A simple smile to a stranger can go a long way, and the same goes for texting a friend to see how they've been doing. This really doesn't cost us anything except perhaps a few seconds. You're showing people that you care, and this is way more valuable.

Think about the things in your life that have changed you in some way, shape, or form. Reflect on your past, but don't let it define you. In life, you take a piece of your experiences with you going forward. Being intentional with what you do and how you do it can change your perspective and actions.

Take Action

Being intentional fits into leadership in numerous ways as well as other fields beyond leadership. Destiny Brandt, founder and CEO of It's Destiny Recruiting, works in sales recruiting. She has worked with plenty of clients, but she is intentional about determining what each client's wants and needs are. Destiny works hard to go beyond the typical business transaction—when she's trying to build relationships with investors, she always likes "to ask them what they look for in a vendor or recruiting partner, or just in someone that they trust and they can build good relationships with." By establishing this at the beginning of the relationship, this enables more transparency in further communication and builds trust between the parties. Destiny not only is intentional when working with her clients, but she's also committed to her team. The way that she interacts with her team of thirteen (and growing) shows how much she truly cares about them.

Oftentimes, when you're passionate about something, you can tell because you're excited to complete certain tasks for it. Rather than putting off the tasks, you're looking forward to diving into them. Leander Howard II, the founder and CEO of Spark Your Resume, is intentional when assigning his team to certain tasks. Leander purposely puts the people on his team in places that align with what they are passionate about "because if you're passionate about it, you're most definitely going to put in work for it...this is natural to you."

In your life, are you in a place where you're able to intentionally do what you love and grow simultaneously? If not, maybe it's time to take a step back, reflect, and pivot.

We are constantly impacted by our environment, whether this consists of the people or the location. Sevara Mallaboeva, a college student at the City University of New York, has realized how her "cultural background plays a lot into [her] personality and where [she is] currently." Since Sevara has had more diverse experiences in her life from being born into a family of immigrants, she believes this is why she is more open-minded. Having experienced struggles and failures growing up, Sevara didn't want to perpetuate this, so it has led her to intentionally "push [herself] to be the best person that [she] can be," and she is grateful for what she has, especially the "opportunities to do well in school, to push past these barriers."

Seek out different mindsets, perspectives, and experiences. You don't have to grow up in any particular family, area, or socioeconomic class to intentionally seek out information and talk with more people about their experiences. By being more cognizant of the diverse range of experiences that people have, this enables you to be more mindful and see things from another perspective rather than just your own.

How does intentionality tie into our lives apart from relationships from work and family? For many people, mentorship is a huge influence on their lives. Having one or multiple mentors is beneficial because you can bounce ideas off of them as well as ask for help, advice, and support if you get stuck, need to pivot, or take a break. For Sergio Flores-Garcia, a recent college graduate, this was not a reality. He didn't have a mentor growing up and had to figure things out on his own. As a first-generation college student, it was difficult transitioning from high school to college, and he knew he wanted to help make the adjustment for other college students easier.

The way Sergio prefers to mentor underclassmen is through the lens of a friend. He is intentional about building authentic relationships with people rather than a typical and transactional mentor-student relationship. While he was describing one of his closest friends who is two years younger and in his professional business fraternity, he talked about how much his friend has grown since he began his college journey. Despite being a role model and mentor to his friend, Sergio has learned a lot from him too. Watching his friend's growth "is so inspiring...I could see myself in him as well." Sergio's willing to help him in any way he can because he knows what it's like to go through the college experience—he is intentional about making his friend's journey a little easier.

Think about what you value. What's one small thing you can do every day to live more intentionally and think about others more than you think about yourself? Picture the people you care about. What's something you can do for them to show your support? By thinking more intentionally about our actions every day, this strengthens this skill. Being intentional once in a while isn't difficult, but being intentional every second is. It's no longer enough to just have pure intentions; you must act on them. Doing so will not only make you a better leader but also a better family member, friend, coworker, and human.

Leaders should be more intentional every day because they are human, and they care about others around them. Intent doesn't always equal the impact you have, but the more you practice being intentional for good reasons, the better you will get at sharing your message with others.

Chapter 5:
Better Together

"One friend can tether us to the universe, can teach us, can guide us out of our darkness better than anything else can."
—*Miranda Hope*[14]

People always say, "We're better together," but what does this truly mean? What does this look like? When I was about to enter college, it felt like every upperclassman I asked for advice said, "Find your community, find your people." Why is it that humans are more adaptable, more capable, more everything-er together, and how does this pertain to leadership?

Together

There's an African proverb that says, "If you want to go fast, go alone; but if you want to go far, go together."

This sums it up nicely. We're better together because humans are meant to work in teams and collaborate. It's

---

14   Miranda Hope, "One Friend | Miranda Hope | TEDxCharlottesville," TEDx Talks, posted on February 7, 2020, YouTube video, 11:01.

incredibly difficult to do something entirely by yourself and without any support, whether this means physical support or mental support from others. UCLA professor Matthew Lieberman states how the human need "to connect socially with others is as basic as our need for food, water and shelter."[15] For better or for worse, part of our survival as a human race is dependent on our ability and need to connect with other humans.

Even if humans didn't need each other to survive, it wouldn't be as fun being alone constantly. You miss out on the fun of working with a team and going through the same shared experiences as well as building the automatic bond created between team members. People who are working in teams will collaborate for 64 percent longer than individuals, resulting in more engagement and more success with their task, as shown by a study conducted by Stanford.[16] Rather than viewing your responsibilities as hard work you have to do, you're more likely to think of them as fun opportunities to collaborate with others.

While talking to someone, let's call her Diana, about her time playing basketball throughout high school and college, she mentioned how important it was to have a support system. This consisted of family, friends, and general people who were willing to be her sound bound whenever she needed them; Diana could bounce ideas off them and talk through any issues or problems that she was facing. Playing sports in college is time consuming,

15   Stuart Wolpert, "UCLA Neuroscientist's Book Explains Why Social Connection Is as Important as Food and Shelter," *UCLA Newsroom*, October 10, 2013.

16   Adi Gaskell, "New Study Finds That Collaboration Drives Workplace Performance," *Forbes,* June 22, 2017.

and it can be hard to manage all the practices and games with classes. Having her support system and basketball community made it easier because Diana knew she wasn't alone; she had people who cared supporting her.

Diana had found her community of people, something we're all looking for. With billions of other people on Earth, you'd think it'd be easy to find and establish a strong community, but it isn't that simple. We are feeling the effects of a loneliness epidemic, and no one knows when it will end. In fact, more than three out of five people are feeling lonely.[17] With such a huge population of humans on the same planet, why are so many people feeling this way?

Imagine you're driving through a rural town. You're trying to get from Memphis, Tennessee to Dallas, Texas, so there are a few towns you've already passed on your journey. Midway there, you end up getting lost, running low on gas, and losing service. You regret your solo road trip and feel alone because no one is there with you experiencing the same feeling of confusion or frustration. Even if you had one close friend who decided to journey with you, you would be able to bounce ideas off of each other and talk to pass the time. You wouldn't be alone with just your thoughts for company.

According to Douglas Nemecek, MD, "Loneliness has the same impact on mortality as smoking fifteen cigarettes a day, making it even more dangerous than obesity."[18] The thing about loneliness is that it doesn't matter who

---

17   Elena Renken, "Most Americans Are Lonely, and Our Workplace Culture May Not Be Helping," *NPR,* January 23, 2020.

18   Nick Tate, "Loneliness Rivals Obesity, Smoking as Health Risk," *WebMD,* May 4, 2018.

is physically nearby; it's all about how mentally connected you feel to others around you. Someone who is in a crowded room full of people can still be lonely. In addition, Emma Seppälä, PhD, studied the importance of social connection in a study conducted by Stanford University. She determined that loneliness, a "lack of social connection," is not only worse for our health than smoking cigarettes, but it's worse than high blood pressure too.[19] Good relationships in our lives protect our bodies and brains because when we feel like there are certain people we can count on, our brains continue functioning for longer. Robert Waldinger discovered how relationship satisfaction was a better indication of future health than cholesterol level.[20]

You may be thinking that this is incredibly important to one's health but wondering how it connects to leadership. When you feel like you belong and are supported by others, you will not feel the detrimental effect of this loneliness epidemic as much compared to someone else who doesn't feel the sense of belonging and support. The sense of belonging is cultivated through a strong team culture, and leadership involves bringing people together and building these social connections while lessening the impact of the loneliness epidemic. Teams are also much more effective when the individuals are willing to invest in each other.

19   Dr. Emma Seppälä, "Connectedness & Health: The Science of Social Connection," The Center for Compassion and Altruism Research and Education, May 8, 2014.

20   Liz Mineo, "Good Genes Are Nice, but Joy Is Better," Harvard Gazette, April 11, 2017.

Support

"People are the ROI of life, and time is the investment. Happiness comes from relationships." —Alfred Mugho

When I was talking with Alfred, a management consultant at PwC, our conversation really stuck with me. Alfred and I are both finance majors, so I understood what he meant by return on investment (ROI). When you invest time in people, what you get back is the people in your life. Whenever you add time, energy, effort, and care into your relationships for those around you, this will strengthen your relationships and build a culture of support. Beyond developing these external relationships, Alfred described how investing in others allows you to also grow internally. "As you learn about others, you learn about yourself, and as you listen to others, you begin to listen to yourself." By investing time and energy into people around you, you are also investing in yourself.

Alfred knows "the people you surround yourself with are so important...to have an effective team, you have to have good chemistry." Without good chemistry and inherent trust, it is difficult to build rapport between team members and delegate tasks as needed. This is one of the reasons why he chose to pursue consulting; he "want[ed] to become a great leader...be able to motivate people and learn how to scale solutions." If your team already has a solid foundation of trust established, it will be much easier to cultivate a bond and exponentially increase productivity.

Humans are inherently social creatures. There is a wide spectrum between introverts and extroverts, but we all crave some form of interaction with others. The people who live the happiest and longest lives are those with the strongest social connection in their communities.[21] Human connection is a beautiful thing—this doesn't have to mean a partner, a family, or kids. A connection to your community could mean a neighbor, a friend, or really anybody who you know will support you at your highest highs but especially your lowest lows.

This is something Jaeda Nelson, a college student at Central Washington University, realized when she was going through a difficult time in her life. Someone close to her had recently passed away, and some people who she had expected to support her weren't there for her. Instead, there was someone who she had not expected who showed up. Put in a similar situation, they understood and supported each other. After this experience, Jaeda learned not to settle in friendships where people aren't there for her when she needs them the most. This is because "oftentimes, we become so empathetic to our peers that we cannot do the same for ourselves. There is so much pressure to love others...that we often aren't taught how to create boundaries and be unapologetic about our needs."

Jaeda is someone who gives people multiple chances in hopes that things will change or she "could do something better to avoid being treated badly again because of [her] need for community and support. Sometimes it is better to be alone in our lows than searching for validation from others. We are deserving of more than what we might be receiving, and it is okay to address that and not feel

---

21   Anne E. Holladay, "Relationships and Social Connections Can Help You Live Longer," *Health and Wellness* (blog), *UPMC*, January 22, 2019.

bad for thinking so...in those lonely moments there are opportunities for other relationships to form that we may have unconsciously blocked ourselves from. If we continue in places that make us feel small, how can we ever experience true and authentic friendship?"

It's so easy to support someone at their high but not at their low. Anyone can say "Hey, you did this really cool thing, and I'm proud of you," but it's much more difficult to say "Hey, I know things are a little tough for you right now, but I support you no matter what, and I'm still proud of you." How often do we get this kind of support when we are having a hard day at school or work, feeling burnt out, or getting overwhelmed by our to-do list? On the contrary, how often do people help us celebrate a grand achievement, like passing an important exam, partaking in a large performance, or winning an award at a competition?

This is not to say that these accomplishments don't matter, but not only should we celebrate and take notice of the small wins in life, but we need to support one another during hardships. Especially when someone is struggling, someone's support can mean the world to them. Leaders recognize this and support others in the most difficult times.

Mentorship

Support is a foundational aspect of leadership since it helps build other important traits of healthy relationships, like trust, consistency, and respect. When you intentionally spend time with the important people in your life, and make time for them in your busy schedule, you begin establishing trust in the other person, consistency in the relationship, and mutual respect for each other.

All of this ties into mentorship. When I asked Tina Zhang, a rising freshman at the University of Pennsylvania, about how she had gotten involved in organizations in high school, such as ASB and FBLA, she mentioned how these activities "have been so pivotal and so life changing for me through the people I've met," including the mentors she had. Not only has she learned valuable and transferable skills like public speaking, event planning, and teamwork, but she's also built meaningful relationships with the people around her.

Tina highlighted two senior girls in ASB, Megan and Sydny—she remembered them driving her home after school because she couldn't drive and didn't have a ride. In the car, Tina asked the two girls questions about their purpose because she was still figuring out her own. Megan's answer stuck out to Tina—a lot of students go to school, but they're dreading it. They don't really want to go to school every day because they don't enjoy it, and the best part of high school is graduating and leaving campus. Megan's why related to this; if she could do something like plan an event or be kind to people every day and give them a reason to want to come to school instead of having to, then her job is done. While looking for mentors, Tina intentionally sought out the upperclassmen in her organizations, and she gained two close friends. Tina mentioned, "One of the greatest aspects of being a young and aspiring leader is that the older people around you almost always want to give you advice and answer any question you may have. It's just a gift of being young; so many are willing to offer mentorship."

Another lesson Tina learned from Megan and Sydny is that the smallest details really do matter. She was on the decor committee helping plan for an upcoming dance with the theme of Atlantis; at first, she was confused as to why they were putting in so many hours into finding specific decorations for the dance—she didn't understand the necessity. Tina was told that all the details matter, even the smallest ones. If you treat every little thing like it is currently one of the most important things to you, although it might be overseen by a lot of people, someone will notice it, and it will mean the world to them. By the time of her sophomore year of high school, Megan and Sydny had graduated, so that year she had other upperclassmen mentors. This is one of the best things about being a mentee—you can learn from anyone, making the possibility of who your mentor is, endless.

When you're looking for a mentor, you can do what Tina did—talk to people who are doing the same thing as you but have more experience. Pay attention to the people around you and find someone you want to learn from. The worst thing they can say is "no," but it would have been an automatic no if you hadn't asked them in the first place. Once you find a mentor, you can learn from their experiences and apply these lessons to your own experiences. As you continue living life, you then pay it forward. As Tina said, "I hope that I can be that Megan to Tina someday." This is powerful. Having such an impact on another person to the extent where they want to be able to impact another person is incredibly rewarding and touching.

Building Habits to Be Better Together

What are some habits we can do every day to be the best we can be individually so we can be even better together? Gradual progress is still progress, and incremental changes are much more realistic and sustainable than huge changes.

Mike Catanese, the CEO and founder of Pogo Eclipse, brought this up when he mentioned how he focuses on improving by 1 percent every day. This small improvement accumulates over time, and by really focusing on his goal of 1 percent, he's able to improve more and more over time rather than initially burning out. Mike says, "It's never too late to be the person you want to become," and I wholeheartedly agree with this. Humans are creatures of habit, yes, but we can always aim to change or improve our habits—it simply just takes time and consistency.

Houston, mentioned in the previous chapter, had a great tip for habits. He stated that rather than trying to flip a "bad" habit to a good one, you could just modify or add something to it and make it better. The example he gave me was for people who find themselves continuously scrolling through their social media for minutes or hours on end (I am guilty of doing this). His recommendation was to add a goal to this—for every three posts you scroll past, you comment something positive on at least one of them. I thought this was a brilliant idea because yes, affirmations are always nice to give to others, but also by flipping it from "bad" to good rather than trying to completely abolish the habit, it is more achievable.

Another important habit we can do every day is be conscious of our time. Time is one of the resources that, once we use, we can never get back. What we decide to do with it depends on us. We want to spend time with people who motivate and encourage us to constantly want to improve ourselves.

"You are the average of the five people you spend the most time with." —Jim Rohn[22]

Think about this for a moment. Who are you spending most of your time with? Are they the kind of people you would want to be either today or in the future? Do these people constantly inspire you to be the best version of yourself?

Are these relationships built on trust, support, consistency? Are they people you can count on for advice and mentorship? Will they be there for you in your highest highs but especially your lowest lows?

People matter, especially because relationships are all about people, and leadership is all about relationships. When you're in leadership, you are working with other people, so invest in them. Care about others, and people will care about you. We're better together because we are in this together. If everyone had one friend who understood the importance of supporting the people around them, we would all be in a better spot. Sometimes it just takes that one person to change our life. Sometimes it will be a person you know, and sometimes it will be you.

---

22   Aimee Groth, "You're the Average of the Five People You Spend the Most Time With," *Business Insider,* July 24, 2014.

Chapter 6:
Inspire Confidence

"A great leader gives other people confidence." —Alyssa Dver

According to the National Science Foundation, each person thinks between twelve thousand and sixty thousand thoughts in a given day.[23] Unless you are incredibly skilled and practiced in being present and clearing your mind, you are thinking of something while reading this.

This leads to a key question: How many of our daily thoughts are about ourselves? It takes practice and experience to think about others and our surroundings more often than ourselves. In our childhood, there is a shift from "me" to "we" that occurs, resulting in less egocentrism.[24] As we age, leaders are able to see potential in others and inspire them to achieve it, especially when they don't see it in themselves—this is how a lot of people

---

23   Neringa Antanaityte. "Mind Matters: How to Effortlessly Have More Positive Thoughts," *Mind Matters* (blog), *TLEX Institute,* accessed March 1, 2021.

24   Healthwise Staff, "Egocentric and Magical Thinking," *Healthwise,* May 27, 2020.

come to realize they are capable of so much more than they originally thought. Before we get to this point, we first need to build confidence in ourselves.

Confidence in Ourselves

Akash Karia is "very much an introvert. And [he] always [has] been." When he was growing up, he used to be very shy; you wouldn't expect this because now he is a keynote speaker who has spoken to thousands of people across the world about how to connect and communicate with others. However, after one incident at school when he was the only person in his class not invited to a class party, he realized he "needed to change the way that [he] communicate[d] with people. [He] wasn't a bad person... and yet it was as if [he] did not exist."

Akash began reading personal development books like *How to Win Friends and Influence People* and *The Art of Public Speaking*. Over time, he realized "there are specific tips, tricks, tactics, mindsets that [he could] use to connect with other people," and over ten years, he built up his self-confidence as he learned how to talk to people and make friends.

By the time he got to university, his social skills were significantly better, and he even joined Toastmasters International, a public speaking club. Members of Toastmasters typically give a speech once every month or so during the club meeting, but Akash went above and beyond this. When he joined, he "emailed all the Toastmaster clubs in Hong Kong to say [he] would love to speak to them. In [his] first year in Toastmasters, [he] gave over 150 speeches," so a speech every two days. As

Akash delivered more and more speeches, he began to win awards and grew passionate about public speaking. After growing up with self-confidence and self-esteem issues, Akash realized he successfully "developed [his] self-confidence, and [he] also learned some tools and tactics along the way," so he wanted to give back and teach other kids social and public speaking skills—this was the beginning of his journey as a speaker.

We all need a bit of self-confidence to be effective leaders. Not only is it easier to resonate with people if we believe in ourselves, but people will also begin to believe in us.

Much like Akash, during my last year at Mt. Adams as a delegate, I faced some self-confidence issues when I was contemplating applying to be a junior counselor (JC) for the following summer. The main role of the JC is to support the high school delegates, and I wasn't sure if I would be a good JC, even though there is no textbook definition. After ruminating over the week of camp, I was leaning towards just applying and giving it a shot. After all, what did I have to lose?

On the second to last day, everyone does an activity called million-dollar paychecks. This is where each person in the council, a group of about fourteen delegates, the senior counselor, and the junior counselor, get a chance to write an individualized note to everyone. Each note is placed in an envelope, sealed, and then given back to the person to read after camp has ended.

The envelopes usually get opened on the bus on the way back home or after the delegate has returned home. I remember opening my own envelope with a bittersweet feeling and heavy heart because of how much I missed everyone. As I slid my finger under the seal and read each person's note, I noticed my SC had written that I should definitely apply to be a JC.

My SC saw potential in me, and although I was scared of letting him or myself down, I knew the answer would be an automatic no if I didn't apply at all. I swallowed my pride and my nerves, filled out my application, and asked my ASB advisor for a reference.

Self-confidence is really interesting because of how much it connects to science. This is something Alyssa Dver, a TEDx Talk speaker, author, and CEO and co-founder of the American Confidence Institute (ACI), described to me. Whenever you're trying to convince another person to do something while they are anticipating being asked to do something, you're both mentally on guard. This is different from when you're presenting information and your audience is just there to learn because "you are just giving information, and there's no expectation" you have for them.

As a result of being on guard, you are less open-minded and don't have as much control of your overall behavior since your body is in reactive mode. If you were to walk into a room ready to pitch a product to an investor, your guard would be up in anticipation. To mitigate this, it's best to approach the pitch with the mindset of sharing a mutually beneficial opportunity rather than selling the investor something, be it yourself or a product. When people successfully do this, "it changes everything. It changes the way people think and approach their pitch, [and] how they walk in the room. They're not as worried about being rejected as they are worried about being able to convince somebody why this is so good for every-body...people are more relaxed...it's still nerve wracking, but they have a lot more confidence that they're there for the right reason."

We all want to take the opportunities that are beneficial—for both ourselves and others. If it takes figuring out why something is mutually beneficial, it'd be worth going the extra mile to boost our self-confidence. This would enable you to persuade someone to take action as well. We must be confidence in ourselves and our "why" before we build confidence in others.

Inspiring Confidence in Others

Looking back, Kelty Pierce, the past president of the Associated Students of the University of Washington (ASUW), could not have visualized her leadership journey from where she began to where she is today. After running for ASB Treasurer in her eighth-grade year and losing, she felt dejected. Upset, she spoke with her mom when she got home later that day. Kelty's mom pointed out that Kelty didn't need the title and "no one cares if you're ASB Treasurer...you can still be involved." This was a good reminder and a confidence boost for Kelty because although she didn't get elected, she still knew she wanted to help leave an impact and serve the student body.

Whether this looked like cleaning up the lunch tables or running a food drive for her school, "seeing a need and being able to meet that need" was Kelty's priority. She didn't let her loss defeat her purpose, and she continued to be involved in her high school's leadership program.

With the support from her mom, Kelty went on to serve in ASB during high school and in ASUW in college.

One of Kelty's favorite quotes from Mt. Adams is, "Leave people in places better than you found them." This connects to what her mom was able to do for her; she lifted up Kelty's spirits and left her in a better place than the one she found her in. When certain expectations and hopes are not met, it can be easy to question your capabilities. Having people around you to remind you of what you are inherently capable of and rebuild your confidence is what leaders do best.

No matter where we are in life, there are potential opportunities we simply are unable to see; thankfully, there are other people near us who can. Brent Grothe's older sister told him, "When you were two years old, you seemed like you knew where you were going. You had a direction in your life. You seemed sure where you were headed even at two years old." Despite this, Brent still needed encouragement to pursue leadership positions. In the spring of his junior year of high school, Brent was sitting in choir. One of the altos came over to him and tapped him on the shoulder, saying "Have you ever thought about running for ASB office? I think you should. I think you'd be good...I think you should run for president." This is what Brent did, and he was elected. Little did he know that this was only the beginning of his lifelong journey in leadership.

When I met Brent at Mt. Adams, the same leadership camp he had attended as a high school student, he was the director at the time. This forty-year leadership journey of Brent's started through one person, the alto in high school choir, acting like a catalyst. She saw the potential in Brent and took the extra step to suggest he run for a leadership position. As Brent put it, "Unbeknownst to her, that suggestion changed the course of my entire life."

Sometimes you will encounter another person who sees the potential in you. Other times, you are the one who is able to see it in other people. For Nahom Azmach, a college student at Western Washington University, his leadership journey began similarly to Brent's. In his case, however, he was encouraged by a teacher. In his sophomore year of high school, he took Introduction to Leadership, a prerequisite for the leadership class associated with ASB. When Nahom's teacher said he should take the leadership class associated with ASB his junior year and run for a position, he did just that and became elected as vice president.

During his junior year, Nahom met someone in his English class who was known for causing trouble. Although he knew this, Nahom was especially aware of the danger of a single story. He decided to talk to him and make up his own opinion rather than just listening to everyone else's. Over time, they became friends and Nahom grew to learn about his friend's story and home life, then encouraged him to also join the leadership class the following year. Despite his friend's initial hesitation, he took Nahom's advice and changed as a person. This change only happened because he wanted to change for *himself*. Originally, his friend didn't envision a future for himself after high school, so when Nahom saw his potential and urged him to take action, he became inspired and took a leap of faith. Taking that one step can move mountains—one step leads to another, which can cause a third, and then a fourth, and a fifth, and so on. Change can be difficult, but it's much more reasonable and realistic in these small steps. You just need to take the first step.

One of the most influential people in John Norlin's life is Brent Berry, someone he got to know while growing up and spending eight summers in Canada with the University of British Columbia's residential hockey school. He started out as a camper, then eventually worked for the school in his later high school years. John was responsible for a group of kids, and it was his first time as a lead instructor. One night, there was a kid who got his feelings hurt by a group of the other kids, so he ended up calling home. John was told that although everything was fine, the family needed to pick their son up and take him home. The next day, the boy's mom came to the rink when they were out on the ice for the morning session, and when John spotted her, he went over to ask how he could help.

The mom started yelling at John, telling him he had no idea what he was doing, and he didn't care about the kids. When she said he didn't care, this really hit him hard because at the hockey school, it was more than just about hockey. Going through training, John was always told that the most important thing was to ask "How can I help?" and to have the mom say he didn't care about the kids was like a punch to the stomach. John started having second thoughts, thinking maybe he didn't know what he was doing and didn't actually care.

A couple of hours later, John received a note saying Brent wanted to talk to him. When John walked into the office, Brent told him he received a call from the boy's mom. John believed he did something wrong and was anticipating getting in trouble. Brent told John "he listened to her until she said that John Norlin doesn't care...in that moment I cut her off and said, 'Excuse me, John really does care. And if I had a kid in this hockey school, I would want him to be in his group.'"

Up until this point, John was ready to go home. He thought he wasn't good at being a lead instructor because the boy's mom had planted a seed of doubt in his head over something he had had no control over—a situation where one kid at a camp gets their feelings hurt because of other kids can happen to anyone. Although John did nothing wrong, he still believed he did.

He realized when you are in a position of leadership, you simply can't please everyone, and he needed to be more confident in his abilities. Things outside of your control will go wrong, and you won't always make the right decision. If John had actually gone home that day, he likely would not have co-founded CharacterStrong, a company that provides character building and social-emotional learning curriculum to teachers and students. He wouldn't be where he is today.

There will be moments in life when we doubt ourselves, and that's normal. We all need people to remind us of what's true and what's false during these times.

Confidence Together

Megan Burch, an elementary school teacher, completed a triathlon in Lake Washington. Incredibly impressive, right? What's even more impressive is that she didn't know how to swim—she was actually terrified of swimming in open water when she agreed to compete.

Megan trained with three other girls for the swimming segment of the triathlon, and she eventually learned how to swim in a pool. Two weeks before the race, they decided to practice swimming the route in the actual lake. It was a difficult training session for Megan because she wasn't used to swimming in open water with waves. When she and the other three girls finished their practice, Megan noticed there was a woman with sunglasses on the shore wearing an orange safety vest. The woman was accompanied by another person in a vest with the word "guide" on it.

They started talking, and Megan found out that not only was the woman training for the same triathlon, but she was also blind. The woman told them "even though she was blind, she knew that she could do it...her disability was no reason for her to give up living life and meeting her dreams." She had always dreamt of doing a triathlon, and she turned her dream and idea into a feasible plan.

Megan felt incredibly touched and inspired. Although training for the triathlon had been a difficult experience between learning how to swim and getting over her fear of swimming in open water, she witnessed the woman's presence, attitude, and determination to complete the triathlon. She was committed to her dream and didn't want anything, including being blind, to get in her way of fulfilling it.

On the day of the race, Megan got to witness the woman come out of the water after she finished the swimming segment with her guide. Megan was sobbing; she "was so moved by the fact that I didn't die in the water, but then seeing [the woman], it was like 'if she can do it, I can do it.'" Megan's friend, an amateur photographer, captured a photo of the woman crossing the finish line, and even though she's a stranger whose name Megan doesn't even know, the picture is framed on her wall.

The woman may never know the impact she had on Megan, but it doesn't mean she is any less of a leader. "Her story changed me...she did it; she crossed the finish line." Just like the woman took that leap, so did Megan, and they both made it past the finish line.

This is an incredible example of how it is very possible to impact people through simply living out your own dreams. You don't need a huge following or a group of people who know your name and background to be a leader. You just need one person. Even if Megan hadn't crossed paths with the blind woman, I'm sure she still would have completed the triathlon, but having someone to look up to pushed and inspired Megan even more.

We are often presented with an opportunity that scares us but will simultaneously force us to grow. Perhaps we would not be where we are today if it weren't for this one person who believed in us and told us we were capable. Maybe someone we know wouldn't be where they are today if we hadn't believed in them and told them they could do it. Either way, we are fully capable of impacting those around us without knowing.

There are going to be moments when we don't believe in ourselves. We are going to face impostor syndrome again and again. Yet, through being intentional about supporting others around us, we can all achieve our potential, especially when we don't see it in ourselves. Try focusing your thoughts outward for a day and reflect on how you feel compared to a typical day. Pay attention to other people and see if they have more potential than they realize. You can help guide their way through a nebulous path and turn it into one that's more straightforward.

Chapter 7:
Strength Redefined

———

"Just keep swimming." —Dory[25]

We all experience difficult moments and emotions in life. Tears. Insecurities. Physical weaknesses. Fears. Judgment. Impostor syndrome. Death. And no, things don't get easier with each occurrence. As human beings, we feel hurt and pain just like any other animal. And that's okay—what you're dealing with is not stronger than you.

We just need to take a step back and understand it's okay to not be okay all the time. If we were always just "okay" and life didn't have its ups and downs, then we certainly wouldn't appreciate the good moments as much. Life happens, and it won't always be sunshine and rainbows. Being vulnerable in these moments is a strength, and it's a necessary part of leadership and life. When we deal with difficult times, we need to remember five things:

———

25 *Finding Nemo,* directed by Andrew Stanton (2003; Emeryville, CA: Pixar, 2013), DVD.

- Vulnerability is a strength

- Be in touch with your emotions

- Understand the difference between sympathy and empathy

- Create a space for yourself and others

- You will get through this

Vulnerability is a Strength

"Vulnerability is not winning or losing; it's having the courage to show up and be seen when we have no control over the outcome. Vulnerability is not weakness; it's our greatest measure of courage." —Brené Brown[26]

Growing up in the United Kingdom, Barnaby has felt the invisible pressures of toxic masculinity. It was not socially acceptable for boys and men to cry because they were supposed to appear strong. One day, Barnaby was having a tough day, and despite being hesitant, he tried something different. In a video, he "talked about...and admitted to crying...[he] was very emotional about it, and it brought up a lot of old trauma and memories." He decided to post it on Instagram because he recognized how he was feeling was not only valid and normal, but by sharing his own experiences on social media, he believed it would help normalize the expression of emotions.

Since then, Barnaby has continued to post other videos on his Instagram account to share with the world. He knows "vulnerability equals strength because if you're

---

26   "Excerpt from Brené Brown's Rising Strong: The Physics of Vulnerability," *Parade*, September 4, 2015.

vulnerable, that means you're incredibly courageous. It doesn't mean you're weak. It means that you're able to transcend societal expectations and be brave enough to get beyond thinking about what people might or might not think." Through posting and bringing awareness to important topics like toxic masculinity, it's become easier for Barnaby to express himself and connect with others on a deeper and more meaningful level.

It's impossible to live life fully without feeling any kind of emotion, from the happiest to the most terrible. This is just the reality of life. Everyone experiences difficulty, and sharing this with others is not easy. However, going through life without sharing what you're going through with others is incredibly lonely.

This is a feeling Madeline Steitz, a Washington State University graduate, felt when she was elected the president of her sorority. She didn't expect that soon after, she would experience a large injury. After the injury, Madeline had to use a walker and ask for help from other people. She struggled to do this because as president, she was "supposed to be seen as the strong person...seen as this person that has it all together." Being wracked with her insecurities telling her she wasn't a strong and reliable leader due to her physical limitations was stressful. Eventually, she realized, "There's so much power in vulnerability and in asking for help. That isn't necessarily talked about a lot."

Being vulnerable is really, really hard. Yet, it's incredibly rewarding when you express how you are feeling or talk about what you're going through rather than avoiding and invalidating your emotions. The thing about vulnerability is that it's something you can practice and be more intentional about in your daily life. When some-one asks you how you are doing, how do you respond? Maybe you say you're "good," "fine," or "doing alright" even when you're not. Trust me, I'm guilty of this too. We don't always feel like unloading our problems on the person or we don't want to get into what we are dealing with. And this can be alright. What's not alright is if we ignore our situation, pretend our issues don't exist, or invalidate our feelings. There is a difference between purposely waiting to address an issue and completely avoiding it.

Be in Touch with Your Emotions

There is a certain power and strength in the written (or typed!) word. Sometimes words are better left unsaid. Unwritten. Untold. Everyone has certain stories they hold close to their hearts and never share with others. During these moments when you want to be raw and open but simply cannot, there are other options.

One of them is writing down or typing up your thoughts. This helps structure the thoughts going through your mind, which helps your brain process them better. Simi-larly to how there's a difference between learning a con-cept and being able to teach it to someone else, there is a difference between thinking something and formu-lating that thought on paper. If you're writing out your thoughts, it's helpful to let everything flow naturally and follow your stream of consciousness. What this means is to write out your thoughts out without any inhibition. This way, you are giving yourself permission to think about anything and everything.

An alternative is to write a letter to someone that you know you're not going to send. This is a method A.J. Hostak, a high school educator, practices. He believes it's a good way to dig deeper into your emotions and thoughts and be as expressive as you want. This can be especially therapeutic for people who have been hurt by others since they can process what happened, how they feel, and hopefully let it go and move on. Of course, if you actually decide you want to send the letter, you can, but going into it knowing the intent is to get your thoughts down gives yourself permission to be honest.

You can also record a video and talk out your thoughts and feelings. This way, you're able to process what is happening in your life better through voicing your emotions. Sometimes when we speak about something that has been on our mind, it helps get it off our chest.

A.J. is not usually one to be vulnerable, especially over technology. However, this changed when his parents got divorced while he was in college. He sent a Facebook message to his friends to share this with them. If given a choice, A.J. would choose to be vulnerable in person, but he felt this time was different. He wanted to be intentional about telling his friends because for where he was in his life and on his late journey of vulnerability, "being vulnerable was not in my repertoire, and so that was a new concept for me. But it was definitely the best thing in my life at that moment to be vulnerable." In his friendships, A.J. focused on establishing trust and authenticity, and this was a time when he really needed his friends to support him throughout this process. A.J. was in touch with his emotions, and he chose to be vulnerable.

Sympathy vs. Empathy

"There's a certain power and magic in conversation when you listen and have empathy." —Andrew Riis

When we're asking others how they are doing, especially when receiving an open and heartfelt response, it's good to remember the difference between sympathy and empathy. Sympathy is just feeling bad for someone while empathy is more like feeling the other person's pain with them. Generally, people don't want others to feel bad for them or to pity them. There's usually not much they can do to change their circumstances anyway.

One prime example of the important distinction between sympathy and empathy is when we are dealing with sick loved ones. When Houston Kraft found out his mom was sick with stage four colon cancer, there were numerous people who reached out to him. They would say words like "I'm so sorry" or "She's going to be okay, she's a tough lady"—really, any of the classic, comforting words you'd expect. These words weren't inherently bad because these people were expressing their thoughts and emotions and trying to help lift Houston's spirits. But the thing is that these words didn't make Houston feel any better.

When Houston was pulled aside by Megan Burch, mentioned in Chapter 6, he braced himself for the same words he'd been hearing. What surprised him was how "Megan didn't say any of them. She just sat with me, looked at me and started to cry, gave me space to cry, and she gave me a big hug. And that was it." Megan's decision to choose empathy, actually feeling what another person is going through, over sympathy, feeling bad for someone else, was "so much more profoundly kind than 'I'm so sorry.'" Especially since Megan was vulnerable first, she essentially gave Houston permission to in turn be vulnerable.

Create a Space for Yourself and Others

Everyone wants to be seen for who they are and not be judged. It can be hard to admit we are hurting and need support because of societal pressures to appear okay all the time. This simply is not realistic, though, and we have to create a safe space for ourselves and others.

After Drew Dudley, author of *This is Day One: A Practical Guide to Leadership that Matters,* lost the woman he loved, he was unable to cry due to trauma. About three months after her death, he found himself driving through Idaho while listening to a storytelling podcast called *The Moth.* The podcast episode, "Facing the Dark," discussed how adults can learn from children in how they deal with death and grief, and a woman in the episode named Kate was sharing her own story about death and loss. She said, "Just remember that grief is just love squaring up to its oldest enemy," and this was when Drew was finally able to cry and grieve.

Even though Drew didn't know Kate personally, she still had an enormous effect on him. She "made it possible for [him] to one, cry, and then two, start to process what had happened three months earlier." Drew believes the reason why this episode affected him so intensely is because the woman was willing to share her story, which helped give Drew permission to actually think about and reflect on his own story in the past three months.

This is why Drew believes "leaders need to put parts of their story out into the world...you do not know who it's going to hit, when it's going to hit them, and why it's going to be important." No matter what your story is, that's *your* story, and by showing strength in character yourself, maybe you'll help people who say "Oh my god, I thought I was the only one" realize they're not actually alone. Drew created a space for himself through listening to the podcast and was able to express his emotions.

It's also important to create a space for others. One of my favorite things to do is FaceTime friends out of the blue and on a whim. If a friend picks up, then fantastic, we'll chat for however long we are both available for. If they don't, then I will call someone else. During these calls, I am intentional about seeing how they are doing—not just how they want to be perceived, but how they *really* are doing. Nahom, mentioned in the last chapter, has a favorite question to ask others, which is "How are you doing, *really*?" This gives the person you're asking a little nudge and permission to say exactly how they are doing rather than just giving the common response of "Good, how are you doing?" Of course, not everyone will want to unload everything they're currently feeling, but this intentionality helps create a space for others to do so if inclined. This strengthens the trust in any relationship because you're actively showing up for others. They know you care for them no matter what.

One moment that has stuck with Joe Beckman, a speaker on the importance of human connection, is one from his senior year in high school. Joe grew up in Minnesota, so his first time riding a subway was on a school trip in Chicago. He remembers how he and his friends were having fun and enjoying the new experience. Then, the brakes squealed, the train stopped, and as the doors opened, a woman walked in. She had a cart with her things in it, and he could tell from this and her demeanor that she was most likely homeless.

It became really quiet in the subway car, and Joe watched as the woman started to cry. He thought to himself that he should do something, but another voice told him not to because "you have nothing to do with this, you have no idea what's going on...this is not your job." Ultimately, Joe ignored the second voice in his head and went over to the woman. He sat next to her, and when she looked at him, he remembers in that quick glance he saw so much hurt, pain, shame, and grief. Joe instinctively put his arm over her and squeezed her shoulder as if to say, "I see you." She "leaned her head into [Joe's] chest and began to weep...deep, heavy cries." Then, the train stopped again, and it was her stop. She got up, gathered her things, and without a word to Joe, exited the train. Joe hasn't seen her since, but he thinks about her and that moment a lot.

Joe created a space for the woman to feel heard, seen, and recognized for who she was. He's not sure how much of an impact he's made on her and whether or not she remembered the moment, but he believes in his heart that "part of our jobs as humans is to make sure that we let others know that they're part of the group...that they belong, that they're seen, that they're known. We might not have long, deep lasting relationships with them, but at the same time we're all sharing the same space, we're all breathing the same air, we're all part of the family." Joe didn't expect anything in return from the woman; he just wanted to show her he cared.

When you think of improvisational theatre, commonly known as improv, is one of the first things that comes to mind comedy? Yeah? Me too. However, for A.J., he remembers when he understood someone and their fears because of improv. A.J. had a friend in college who he met through doing improv together. Once when they were paired together for an activity, they were tasked with sharing their fears in life. Although this was no easy feat, A.J. remembers his friend "sharing he was fearful he would never end up with someone else" in a romantic relationship. This really impacted A.J. because it truly is "so powerful when someone allows themselves to be vulnerable and open and just let go of that guard...take off the mask." It's moments like these when we remember how human everyone is. No matter what, there are certain fears people have, both rational and irrational. Improv allowed A.J.'s friend to be vulnerable, and A.J. listened and held space for him.

Continuing on the thread of how doing something first enables and allows others to be more open, Michael Larson, a college student at Gonzaga University, has suggestions for creating a safe place for vulnerable conversations:

1. Step one: The time and the place are incredibly important.

    Conversations usually can't happen at the breakfast or lunch table because people are in a rush; they have stuff on their minds. Nighttime is the best time to have these conversations because people's walls are lower, and there's fewer time limits on conversations.

2. Step two: You need to be the one who goes first. Any vulnerable conversation needs to start with the person who wants to have it. A lot of people don't know how to initiate vulnerable conversations, so by going first, you set the tone.

Remembering the structure of these steps can allow for more vulnerable conversations. The way Michael thinks about this is that if you're in a pool in the three-feet section and this is where you take the conversation (the surface level area), people will only meet you there. However, if you're willing to jump into the deep end, people will still swim over to meet you there.

Rather than going out on a limb and being vulnerable first, we prefer to stay in our comfort zone unless prompted—when someone takes the first step themselves, it is easier to be vulnerable in return.

You Got This

"What separates a leader from the rest is that they're not willing to give up, and they're willing to keep going, no matter what." —Caitlin Logue

When Claire started her freshman year of college at Gonzaga University, she had a rocky start. She struggled finding the vital aspect of community because her friend group was more surface level and condescending. She didn't feel valued. During the year, she and her friends made plans to live together the following year, but then Claire found out the four other girls had actually planned on living without her and just didn't tell her.

They thought it would be easier to find two additional people for a group of six than have Claire and find one more roommate. This is when Claire "felt zero value in that moment...felt pretty beat down because these girls were the best friends I had at college."

When she talked about what happened with other friends she had made, Claire realized how blind she'd been to how terribly these girls treated her. Once she understood those friends weren't the best people for her, she began to get closer to another friend in her leadership program as well as their friend group. This took a lot of courage because Claire needed to be open and vulnerable. Now living together, Claire has noticed how transparent, vulnerable, and honest her new friends are. She recognized "how grateful [she] was to have people who gave me value, who made me feel confident, who were constantly uplifting me, but who also weren't scared to tell me when they were frustrated, when they were grieving, when they were annoyed with me."

Recognizing the terrible situation she was in with her old friend group and walking away took courage and strength. Being able to then put herself in a vulnerable spot by becoming friends with someone new also took courage and strength. Later reflecting on her experiences and understanding what it looks like to have genuine friends unafraid to be vulnerable took courage and strength.

In life, there will be friendships and people who aren't the best for you. They don't encourage you to be the best version of yourself and instead make you feel terrible about yourself. This is when you need to leave and find something better.

Mental and emotional strength look different from physical strength; sometimes we need to take life day by day. Ask for help when you need to and remember there are people by your side. We all are strong people—stronger and more capable than we think. This is not because we always handle what life throws at us or because we think we have our lives together but because even when we don't think we can get through something, we try anyway. We do the best we can in the space created for us. The ways in which we lead are cultivated by our experiences, and we need to be able to accept our own stories and ourselves for what they are and who we are without judgment.

By allowing ourselves to be vulnerable, we encourage others to do the same. This collective vulnerability strengthens the bond between people in a team, but practicing vulnerability enables you to be more in touch with your and others' emotions, which results in being a better leader.

Life can be tough, but you are tougher. Remember this, give yourself grace, and embrace vulnerability.

Chapter 8:
Failing is Good

———

"If you don't fail, you just don't learn." —Jesús Hijas, author of Unleadership: Hacia un Liderazgo más Humano en tiempos de Inteligencia Artificial

Failure is a quintessential part of life, no matter who you are and where you are. One of the best parts about failure is you can bounce back from it, grow, and end up even better than where you had started.

Failure

As I was walking down the hallway, I felt an immediate sense of déjà vu. Here I was again, only a year later, about to interview for a summer internship with the Port of Seattle. The main difference this time around was how I vaguely recalled where I was supposed to go, so my steps were a little more confident. It was April 2019, and I was walking as quickly as my black flats allowed with a few minutes to spare. I was nervous and slightly stressed out.

Last year, I had been in this same spot and hadn't made it past the interview stage—I was hopeful things would be different this time.

When I found out last year, I was pretty crushed. I wasn't sure where I had gone wrong in the interview and constantly wondered what I could have done differently; I thought I had failed. But I wasn't done yet. It took some time after this setback to regain confidence in myself and my abilities, but I reached out to a local business to ask if I could intern for them over the summer instead. I had done a mock interview with the founder of the business a few months prior and thought it would be a great learning experience. Thankfully, my request was accepted as a weeklong job shadow, and I learned more than I could have imagined.

Looking back now, I'm glad I got rejected the first time around—this experience heavily impacted me, and I ended up writing one of my college essays about how I was able to remain resilient and take initiative despite failing. Failure can teach you more about yourself than success can. If I had gotten the summer internship the first time around, I wouldn't have realized how driven I was. Reaching out to the local business forced me out of my comfort zone, and I don't think getting the internship offer the second year would have been as meaningful if I hadn't initially failed.

My point is that so many people, myself included, are afraid of failing. We don't want to disappoint people and fall short of expectations, whether this is from ourselves, friends, family, or communities. There's a negative connotation with failure because it's associated with not being good enough, not trying hard enough, not working hard enough, and the list goes on. Although there can be an overwhelming and unbearable amount of pressure to succeed, failure is prevalent in our lives—it's time to realize it's okay to fail. Everyone does, especially when trying something new.

Failure is incredibly common. Millions of people fail at accomplishing their New Year's resolutions because 92 percent of people who set them don't follow through.[27] This means there is an 8 percent success rate, and with the United States population of approximately 330 million people, assuming half of the total population will create resolutions, this results in over 150 million people failing every year.

Prior to starting his company and creating the magical world of Disney, Walt Disney, the visionary of The Walt Disney Company, was fired from his job at *The Kansas City Star* for "lacking imagination and having no good ideas."[28] Fast forward a few years, and Disney is known by millions of people around the world. Being able to fail, pick yourself back up again, and then continue pushing forward requires perseverance. Especially when you know you have a good idea, keep going regardless of how many people tell you no.

"I think it's important to have a good hard failure when you're young... Because it makes you kind of aware of what can happen to you. Because of it I've never had any fear in my whole life when we've been near collapse and all of that. I've never been afraid." —Walt Disney[29]

27 Rachel Schwantes, "Science Says 92 Percent of People Don't Achieve Their Goals. Here's How the Other 8 Percent Do," *Inc. Magazine*, July 26, 2016.

28 India Gladstone, "Here's What the World's Most Successful People Think about Failure," *Gentleman's Journal,* accessed March 1, 2021.

29 Ibid.

Think Big Picture

We all live in our respective bubbles of comfort, which stagnates growth when we stay there for too long. There should be less of an emphasis placed on failure and more on the effort you exert, the fact that you've tried your hardest, and how much you've learned during the process. Giving it all you have in the moment is all you can ask for—you can't really expect anything more than your best. What matters most is you get back up and either try again or pivot. As we continue the cycle of trying, failing, and learning, our "best" evolves into something even greater.

When Mike Catanese, also mentioned in Chapter 5, was a collegiate athlete, he would not have expected his future to pan out the way it did. Mike was on track for going professional and playing in the National Football League, but then he suffered an intense injury. It was the kind of injury that ended the rest of his sports career.

During this time, Mike had to undergo physical therapy to get back into a suitable condition. He was struggling with his mental health; everything had happened so suddenly that he felt like he lost a part of his identity when he learned he couldn't play sports anymore. Although it took time to mentally and physically heal, Mike understood there wasn't much he could do about his situation. He couldn't control or change the past, so he had to accept his situation and move forward.

A similar point came up during my conversation with David Robertson. David asked me if I had ever learned how to ride a bike, and I told him yes. Then, he asked if I ever fell off, and I said I did.

"Did you get back on?" he continued.

"Yup," I replied.

"What drove you to do that? What drove you to get back on the bike in spite of the pain that you felt when you fell?" he pressed.

I told him "I was probably pretty determined to learn how to ride a bike." Then, David said something that made so much sense, yet it was so profound.

"I'll tell you what it was. It's because you probably envisioned what it was going to be like when you and your friends were riding in the park together down the road. How cool it was going to be and how much freedom you were going to have once you learn how to do this. That's [being] vision oriented. It was the vision driving you, not the actual mechanics of learning how to do it. If you had no vision, no desire to ride a bike, but I told you to learn how to do it, as soon as you fell over, you'd be ready to quit. It's too difficult, this is hard, I'm going to get hurt. But once you have a vision of where you want to go, all of a sudden, things can begin to change, and you're going to dust yourself off and you're going to get back on the bike, and you're going to keep going."

I thought this was a jarring concept. Humans were a lot more future oriented than I had thought, even subconsciously. What drives and motivates us to continue may not be where we currently are at (the pain when we fall off the bike) but our vision of where we will be in the future (effortlessly cruising on the roads with friends and having a blast). It's all about the perspective and flipping our brains to think differently. Rather than focusing on where we stand now, why not think about the future and our potential? Once we have a clear idea of where we want to be, we can work backwards and think about the steps we need to take in order to get there.

"The more clear and more robust that vision is, the more solid your path will be to get there." —David Robertson

Think of all the potential ways you can fail. Problems or issues that may arise. Obstacles that you foresee happening. Write them down on a piece of paper and brainstorm ways to mitigate them. There you go, you now have considered big picture problems and you have ways to combat them if they do happen.

One of the best pieces of advice Ari Zucker, a relationship manager for learning solutions at LinkedIn and TEDx Talk speaker, has gotten is to "always think like an executive." After Ari graduated from college and was working his first job, he realized he wasn't sure what was happening. He was new to the company, thus sorely confused, and it took courage and vulnerability for him to admit this to his mentor because he thought he was expected to understand everything already. When he told his mentor about his situation, he sat Ari down for twenty minutes and explained it to him—this is when Ari realized something. He was too focused and zoomed in on his situation. Of course he wouldn't be expected to know everything as a recent college graduate who's new to the workforce and company. This realization has "given [him] a lot of perspective into how problems that seem crucial to [him] actually don't matter and how what [he's] supposed to do fits into the greater puzzle...and [he] think[s] that's helped [him] develop leadership, develop an understanding, and develop strategic thoughts."

After that day, Ari always looks through other people's perspectives and focuses on the bigger picture rather than getting stuck in the little details. This isn't to say that the little details don't matter, but when you're trying to understand something, it can help to zoom out and look at it from a different angle. He also realizes it's okay to not know the answer to everything; what's more important is that he asks for help when he needs it.

Learning from Failure

"Giving up is the greatest failure." —Jack Ma[30]

Even when you think you're about to fail, you might surprise yourself. David Goggins, ultramarathon runner, motivational speaker, retired Navy SEAL, and commonly known as the toughest man in the world, came up with the 40 percent rule: When your mind is telling you that you're done, that you're exhausted, and that you cannot possibly go any further, you're only actually 40 percent done. Many limitations are mental because physically, you're more capable than you would think.[31]

Yash Bhatia, a university student at University College London and podcast host of *The Mindful Youth*, was inspired by David when he ran four miles every four hours for forty-eight hours straight, totaling to forty-eight miles. Yash decided to try this out; he ran so much his knee got injured when he was at the twenty-four-mile mark. Despite the pain, Yash continued to run

30 "'If You Don't Give up, You Still Have a Chance. Giving up Is the Greatest Failure,' Says Jack Ma Yun," *The Silicon Review*, May 31, 2018.

31 Peter Economy, "Use the 40 Percent Rule to Break through Every Obstacle and Achieve the Impossible," *Inc. Magazine*, April 23, 2019.

until the thirty-six-mile mark and walked the remaining twelve miles to meet his goal. Powering through and resisting the urge to give up is challenging. If it were easy, everyone would do it. However, it is crucial to understand where your breaking point is because even if you don't want to give up, it is occasionally in your best interest to do so. Yash was injured for the next month, and I personally would recommend waiting until you're healthy again before continuing a physically intensive activity, even when you're mentally capable.

Why isn't failure more normalized? It's always great to celebrate our successes, but isn't it more important to focus on the times we've failed so we can take the time to reflect and learn from these moments?

In psychology, the definition of learning isn't just realizing something new. It is a "relatively lasting change in behavior that is the result of experience."[32] Although it is difficult to experience *everything* the world has to offer, we can talk to other people who have had unique experiences we are interested in learning about.

Particularly when you're a student, professionals are happy to schedule a time to chat for you to learn from them and their experiences compared to if you were a fellow working professional. This concept is something commonly known as the "student card." Taking advantage of this opportunity is always something I recommend. Although formal education does stop at some point, we're hopefully all students for life, and Kendra words this nicely below.

---

32 Kendra Cherry, "The Psychology of How People Learn," *Verywell Mind*, May 28, 2020.

"When you think of learning, it might be easy to fall into the trap of only considering formal education that takes place during childhood and early adulthood: but learning is realistically an ongoing process taking place throughout all of life."
—Kendra Cherry[33]

There are still ways to connect with different people and learn from them even when you're no longer a student. The Internet has proved to be an invaluable tool, and it really is just a matter of reaching out and being willing to meet others through various community groups. Aside from talking with others, there is also information at our fingertips. When it's challenging to find new people to learn from, you can always search for information online.

By staying open to learning new things, this enables you to gain more knowledge and be less susceptible to failing. You tend to think more broadly, helping to catch problems and find potential solutions. When you do fail, take a step back and reflect on what happened, how it happened, and why it happened, then most importantly, what you learned from it. People often give up after one failed attempt at learning or trying something for the first time. Having a growth mindset is essential because you will continue to fail again and again.

When you're learning something new, it's important to recognize that other people may have different opinions. Diana, previously mentioned in Chapter 5, says "everybody has their own opinions, and there's not always one right answer." Even if other people are trying to convince you that your method is incorrect, don't succumb to the pressure of groupthink. If everyone in the world had the

---

33 Ibid.

same values and perspectives, life would be pretty boring. What you want is people "from diverse backgrounds, from all over the place, and everyone grows up a little differently." This diversity in thought helps promote growth and challenges everyone to collectively think deeper. When working with others, "embrace being different...but respect others as well." Being completely set in your ways abandons the goal and benefit of collaboration. Instead, finding a balance between understanding what you think and staying open to what others believe is mutually beneficial and helps keeps the communication between the overall team strong.

This reminds me of something I had learned in a nutrition class I had taken in college. My professor proposed that instead of abstaining from eating any more chocolate or ice cream for the rest of your life, which can be quite difficult for people (I know it'd be tough personally), you can add something healthy to it, like nuts with the chocolate or fresh fruit as ice cream toppings. This way, you're able to enjoy something tasty and not feel like you have to omit it from your life since it's not completely unhealthy for you. By doing this, it's also giving you back more control over your actions and allows for more options and flexibility. This whole concept is similar to thinking with a "yes and" mindset rather than a "but" mindset. When you're working with others, adding to their ideas is most likely a better option than immediately rejecting them.

Learn from your past experiences as a leader to be an even better one moving forward. Even when we have failed or think we are about to, this doesn't equate to us being failures. Failing forces us to think and act quickly, and if there is one thing I've learned, it's that when one door closes, there are five more that open. You just need to be watching out for them so you can recognize them when they appear. It is expected to fail at some point—everyone does, and it's just a matter of when and how. What's critical is that we learn from our failures so we can better navigate the waters ahead rather than crashing. When we sometimes do crash, we take a moment to reset rather than allow it to stop us forever.

Chapter 9:
Work with Others,
for Others

"Coming together is a beginning, staying together is progress, and working together is success." —*Henry Ford*[34]

Working with others can be difficult because everyone thinks and acts differently. At the same time, it is incredibly rewarding when you are able to create something with others. In stressful moments, remembering that we are more similar than we are alike is key, as well as maintaining open communication, seeking to understand others, accepting feedback, and observing those around us.

Occasionally, you will find yourself being rushed into a position of leadership. This is what happened to Abi, who was mentioned previously in Chapter 1. In his junior year of high school, he and another student co-founded the Technology Student Association (TSA) club. As president, this was Abi's first time in such a high position

---

34 Ulrike Linnig, "Collaboration Is Hard!" *Climate-KIC*, May 24, 2019.

of traditional leadership, and he found himself learning "how to be not only a good leader but an efficient one" as the year continued.

He reached out to one of his good friends, the president of another school's TSA club, for advice and support, and this was incredibly helpful because Abi realized the importance of asking others with similar experiences for help. Although he hadn't previously developed these skills, he and his co-founder worked hard to build the foundation of TSA at their school and properly advertise it to students. Starting something, whether it is a new club or a personal passion project, from scratch is the best way to learn and gain new skills. There are countless times when leaders are put in a situation where they have to step up and learn as they go.

Communication

One summer, one of my interviewees was working at a summer camp with young teens in California. The goal of the camp was to instill leadership skills in the students, and there were a variety of activities they could participate in. One activity was a low ropes course where students had to get from one side to the other while blindfolded. A group ran into an issue when emotions were running high because everyone was frustrated, so a group of girls stepped up and bluntly stated "no one's listening right now." The students knew that since they were blindfolded, open communication was especially important. Before the group made a decision together, they made sure to hear everyone's ideas and that no one was being left out of the conversation. This is relevant in leadership because it's rare to be working individually on a project. You will likely be working with people you don't know well, and to build a strong working relationship, or any relationship for that matter, there needs to be open communication.

Without open communication, we jump to assumptions solely based on our knowledge. Debbie Brooks, a senior training manager, has done this. About five or six years into her career, Debbie had believed her manager to be "a huge advocate for me and was ready to help me take on additional responsibilities and give me new opportunities." This belief was tested when Debbie found out she was passed over for an opportunity to relocate to Dallas to work on software projects she thought she was a great fit for. Upset by this outcome, Debbie didn't communicate with her boss for two weeks.

With time, Debbie calmed down; her boss came to her and told Debbie they needed to talk about what she had in mind for her. Debbie found out that there was an even greater opportunity coming up. Since Debbie hadn't known about this opportunity, she had assumed her boss didn't value her and see her potential at the company when it was actually the opposite. Debbie reacted to the information she did know and now recognizes how "especially in the moment, we get very caught up in how we feel and how we react that it's hard to maintain a clear mind."

"Sometimes you can't see the forest or the trees." —Debbie Brooks

When working with other people, you won't be able to see the big picture if you've only been given half of the puzzle pieces. Communication is important so everyone is on the same page, and refrain from making quick assumptions because you won't always have all the information. By staying level-headed (much easier said than done, I know), it allows you to inquire whether you're missing some crucial information, and then take the appropriate next steps.

Georgia Park, a university student at the University of Technology Sydney and podcast host of *Flip Side Fluent*, was working on a project called Interchange with eight other universities across Australia. It was their first virtual project that consisted of three-hour seminars over Zoom. The time zone differences within Australia were already pretty drastic, and some of Georgia's team members for the project were in other locations around the world. There was one person who was in India, and Georgia recognized it wouldn't be reasonable to "expect him just to wake up when we wake up." Instead, communication and flexibility were needed where those who were awake would work and everyone else would fill in once it was morning in their respective time zones—it was much easier to work with them rather than against them.

Understanding Others

"Seek first to understand, then to be understood."

—*Stephen Covey*[35]

Deke Copenhaver, the former mayor of Augusta, Georgia, knew younger generations had the lowest voting turnout amidst the other age groups. He also recognized how this was the most important age demographic to speak

---

35   Stephen Covey, *The 7 Habits of Highly Effective People: Powerful Lessons in Personal Change* (New York: Free Press, 2004), 247.

to about the importance of voting and politics—Deke intentionally spoke with people from these categories to understand why they weren't voting. Over his term, he made sure to speak at high schools to reach more students and adjusted his speeches to fit his audience better.

One day, Deke ran into a young lady. She was in her teens and "never cared about politics or local government" until she heard him speak fourteen years ago. While talking to her, he learned he was the first person she had voted for. Deke had invested in interacting with younger people because he knew there was a tendency for them to not vote, but he wanted to change this. Years later, he realized the impact of his actions. This is a prime example of delayed gratification. Although you may not immediately see the benefits of understanding others and where they are coming from, it'll always be worth the wait.

Understanding others is one thing Stephen Edvi is intentional about, especially when he was coaching speed skating. Stephen recognized how "kids hate being bossed around...[they] will literally make your life terrible if you're trying to tell them what to do and they're not down to do it," so his method was to have the kids be as involved in the process of learning speed skating as possible.

As a tall individual at six foot two, working with young kids who are around three foot can result in them feeling incredibly intimidated. Stephen made sure to kneel down so he and the kids were at the same eye level, and he asked them what they thought to include them. Purposely including people who are used to being excluded from important decisions makes a huge difference, especially little kids. You're granting them a seat at the table *and* a voice. Ultimately, Stephen's goal was to demonstrate how he is just a skater too, like the kids he coached. He may have a little more experience, but this is the only difference.

When Stephen told the kids he was leaving at the end of the season, he realized how much of an impact he had on them. The kids created a giant scrapbook of pictures from when Stephen began teaching them to more recent times. The scrapbook proved the kids wanted to create a meaningful gift for him. There was also a trophy they gave Stephen that said best coach ever, which he thought was an awesome addition. When you give to others, no matter what it looks like, you'll usually get something unexpected in return. The kids Stephen coached knew he took the time to understand them and cared what they thought.

Rather than thinking as a leader, you have to be at the front leading others, pushing yourself to think differently. You can lead from the middle and from the back just as well, if not better. Thus, Stephen understands that "you always have to adapt, and you always have to be learning...when a leader assumes that they're the best and can do everything...they'll just turn into a dictator." Rather than trying to be the best, it's more important to aim towards continually being the best version of yourself; this will allow for growth within you and those around you.

Feedback

"We have two ears and one mouth so that we can listen twice as much as we speak." —Epictetus[36]

When we are given feedback, we need to be receptive. It is our duty to listen, even if we don't agree with it. It is impossible to please everyone, but taking the time to listen is important. This is when we need to view things from their perspective and try to understand where they are coming from.

A.J., mentioned earlier in Chapter 7, views feedback as "another form of communication," whether it's positive or negative. Part of the reason why he chose to become a teacher is because when he was a student, other students told him he should consider it because he was such a good listener. This was clear to others, but A.J. had not considered this before.

Once we have been given feedback, we can incorporate it into our lives. When trying to listen to others better, Silvie Alnas, a learning specialist, recommends taking it slow. This way, "when you find that you again have lost focus and forgot to listen, do not beat yourself up. Just stop for a second, accept it has happened, praise yourself that you have noticed it, and promise yourself you will pay more attention next time." By being less harsh on yourself for mistakes that occur, it will be easier to accept and incorporate feedback you receive. When you come across a video or article with helpful tips and advice on

---

36 "We Have Two Ears and One Mouth So That We Can Listen Twice as Much as We Speak," *Cornell University Urban Semester* (blog), *Cornell University,* October 19, 2011.

what you're trying to improve, do not immediately discount it and assume it will not be useful. Instead of thinking "Nothing new here, I already know this," be open and watch the video or read the article with an open mind. Perhaps there are new tips you haven't discovered yet, and it's always good to be reminded of what you're aiming toward.

When providing feedback to others, there is one critical thing to remember: attack ideas, not people. If we approach giving feedback like telling someone they are inherently bad because of something they're doing, they will immediately react defensively. If we separate the person and the action, then critique the action, people will respond more favorably.

Collaboration

Collaboration is essential to leadership because of how often you're placed in teams. It's also a key aspect of life—we are better together, after all.

Grant Dever, author of *Lead The Future: Strategies and Systems for Emerging Leaders*, is someone who strives to be involved in his community. He benefits from having "a clear social function, particularly when collaborating with others." Grant was the second employee hired at the Barbara J. Burger iZone at the University of Rochester, so co-founding, launching, and leading the program was a meaningful experience. The purpose of the iZone was to cultivate a community that would encourage undergraduates to pursue their entrepreneurial ideas. Both Grant and the director of iZone, Julia, had the creative autonomy to imagine and execute their vision for the program.

When Grant realized hiring students to co-create the program would ensure they were building a program designed for meeting students' needs, he hired thirteen part-time students.

There were various novel events that didn't exist before iZone, such as the key homecoming called "Meliora Weekend" hosted in their 12,000-square-feet, freshly renovated space. Grant remembered how much time and effort the students managing the event put into it. During the event, there was a pitch competition where the University of Rochester trustees sat on a panel and listened to students pitch their business ideas; the trustees offered constructive feedback and access to resources. The pitches ranged from a plan to expand the access to hearing aids in Africa to creating an Uber for babysitters at the university. The donors loved the pitches, and the former chairman of the Board of Trustees pledged to donate an additional $50,000 to ensure the program would continue. It's immensely gratifying when a team is on the same page and successfully works together to drive impact. Being able to witness this firsthand gave Grant a clear view of what collaboration looked like at its finest.

Another common form of collaboration is a relationship or marriage. This is what Michael Bunch, a sales executive at First Orion, immediately thought of when I asked him a question regarding his most fulfilling experiences—marriage. Due to his realizations from his own marriage, Michael thinks that oftentimes, people believe their partner is going to fulfill the needs they're lacking when in reality, "you're already equipped with everything you need...This person who you're marrying, they can't really fulfill any of your needs." You already have a brain, a body, food, water, shelter, and the rest of what you need to survive.

There are important components of a relationship, like companionship and friendship, but Michael believes these to be more wants than needs because we won't die without them. To him, a lot of people confuse needs and wants, so they project their wants, mislabeled as needs, onto their partners. What happens next is "when that person falls short and doesn't provide what are misconceived as needs, then it creates this vicious cycle" where one person believes they're being mistreated. This results in them treating their partner poorly in turn, and it's a downward spiral from there.

However, if you can come into a relationship with the mindset that you truly have everything you need and your partner will provide you with wants, you will be better off. This connects to group collaboration because when you have certain expectations for your group, you need to communicate this to them. Otherwise, it can be unclear what is a want versus a need. If your needs are not being fulfilled, you will not be as happy.

Observation

Observing how we and other people act in certain environments is necessary for leadership, whether this is for reflecting or improving oneself. Kenar Haratunian, a student at Tufts University, helps teach a class called Netflix and Networking: Leadership Through the Lens of TV. This class is offered to freshman students, and it encourages them to learn strategies for productive self-reflection, helping them recognize how they are leaders in their smaller communities and the greater society. Kenar has the students observe TV characters and analyze how effective they are as leaders. They apply the knowledge and lessons to themselves by focusing on particular traits like empathy, kindness, and authenticity. Kenar's goal is to have the freshmen "start this process of self-reflection, so by the time they go through their years at Tufts and beyond, they understand how leadership development works."

One recent TV show assigned was *The Good Place*, where the characters aren't leaders in the traditional sense. The main characters are able to self-reflect, recognize their room for growth, and build relationships with each other. Using TV shows for the purpose of the class allows students to recognize each character's actions and understand their reasoning behind them. The main topic that week was about finding belonging and being authentic in certain environments, since one of the main characters in the show Eleanor Shellstrop struggled between fitting in and being her authentic self.

This has been a fun opportunity for Kenar to provide a safe environment for the freshmen at Tufts to be their own authentic selves. Especially as a freshman, there is a lot of pressure to only portray the "best parts of yourself...you want to hide the parts that you think other people might not like," which means it's difficult to build a sense of belonging, especially when adjusting to a new environment with strangers.

Just like how you can observe TV show characters for growth opportunities and understand where they're coming from, you can do the same thing with people in your own life. Being self-aware is also an important trait, and by watching others, it helps build a habit where you're observing the people around you and then reflecting on your own life.

When working with others, it's easy to forget your values and act purely based on emotions when you get caught up in the moment—during these times, your decisions are based on what you think rather than what you know. Remembering why it's important to work with other people is grounding. Watching a successful team work together reminds us of what people can accomplish when they are actively communicating, trying to understand each other, and accepting feedback, and observing themselves and their surroundings. There will be countless moments when you're tasked with working in a team, so work with others for the benefit of everyone.

Chapter 10:
Listen with Your Heart

———

"If you don't have soft skills, hard skills don't mean sh*t. Period. It doesn't matter how many degrees you have [or] how many certificates you have. If you don't have the soft skills, you can't execute any of the knowledge that you know. So work on the soft skills." —Dakota Rader

Picture this: You're on your laptop editing your resume and racking your brain to think of the soft skills you've developed over the many years of formal education for your bullet points. You've already included the strong action verbs at the beginning of each bullet point like everyone suggests, but you're struggling to build the rest of it. The primary technical skills you want to highlight, like Microsoft Word, are already showcased; it's just the soft skills you're trying to figure out.

If you've written a resume before, you know exactly what I'm talking about. It's easier to write the technical skills you've gained as opposed to the soft skills, like teamwork and leadership, because they stem from firsthand experiences. It's much harder to teach someone soft skills because it's not something you can spell out to another person if they aren't already familiar with it. There's no instruction guide that comes with soft skills; it requires awkward stumbling and tripping as you go, but the more you practice, the better you get at it.

Just Be

"Sometimes you just need to be present for someone while they're in pain, and it's okay to feel their pain." —Jennifer Macaulay

I first met Jennifer Macaulay, a senior counselor (SC) at Mt. Adams and the founder of Macaulay Consulting, during the summer of 2017. She was my high school group's SC, so she led the school group activities over the week. Frankly, I don't remember what we did that summer or even during the following summer when she was our school group's SC again. What I do remember is how Jennifer has the ability to touch people's hearts just by being her authentic self.

A big fan of Brené Brown, Jennifer not only taught Brené's principles as a part of the Mt. Adams curriculum but did her best to live them out herself. She recalls one summer at Mt. Adams when there was a video shown in the auditorium about empathy. In the video, "one of the things that was really great about [it] was the whole idea of just being present with someone, not trying to fix it, not trying to find the silver lining." Jennifer considers herself the kind of person who tries to fix problems for others by finding silver linings rather than being present with them.

A couple days after Jennifer watched the video, there was an evening discussion about some heavier topics, including suicidal thoughts, and the SCs knew there would be some kids more impacted by the deep topic. As everyone was leaving the auditorium, Jennifer made sure to stand near a light so she could still see kids' faces as they walked by her.

She noticed one kid walking by who was shaking and sobbing. Jennifer "walked up, [she] put [her] arm around him, and [she] said 'It's okay.'" Aside from this, she didn't say anything to him. All they did for the next few minutes was walk around campus in a loop. One of his friends was worried about him, so they joined their walk. By the third loop, the boy had stopped shaking and his breathing had calmed down. Jennifer turned to him and said, "It hit a little too close to home, didn't it?" and he looked at her and said, "Yeah."

They walked for a little longer, and then when they got to his cabin, he said, "I'm going to be okay now." Jennifer turned to his friend and asked, "You're going to stay with him, right?" His friend agreed, and Jennifer gave the boy a hug and walked away. Since it was late at night, Jennifer never knew exactly who the boy was. On the last day of camp, he walked up to her, giving her a big hug.

This was a powerful moment for Jennifer because she was following a technique that was unnatural to her; she didn't try to fix the problem, she just let him be and his thoughts ruminate. Stunned by the power of being in the present, Jennifer realized how impactful human presence can be. Accepting someone's struggles is difficult because they are usually people we care about—we don't want to watch them suffer. But this is not always something we can control. The most we can do in these circumstances is show them we support them and are there for them, even if we can't alleviate their problem.

When people face obstacles, this is when they are able to learn about themselves and other people. Georgia, as mentioned in the previous chapter, moved from England to Australia just shy of her eleventh birthday. She initially thought it wouldn't be too difficult of a transition because they were both English-speaking countries, but she realized it would be harder than expected because of small things like basic Australian geography, popular TV shows other kids have watched, and cultural humor. Georgia knew "in England, [she] lived in quite a small town, and [her] primary school was sixty people in total." After she moved, there were already one hundred people in her year.

One of the first people she remembered meeting after she moved to Australia was a stranger named Warren. Georgia was whale watching, and he was the first proper Aussie she had met. Something that stood out to her about him was his go-with-the-flow mentality and how he "had such a great outlook on life," which was different from what Georgia had grown used to living in England where things are more rigid. She appreciated his energy and how he lived a "simple life but such a happy life."

The more we talk to other people and work with them, the more we are able to humanize them. It's not always easy to accept others for who they are, rather than how we want them to be, but it's certainly an important part of leadership. Knowing you can't always control your and other people's situation is critical to being able to accept yourself and others. If you're trying to change things outside of your control, you'll never be happy.

Just Do

When you're in a position of leadership, assumptions begin to get made about the kind of person you are. This is something Tom Kolditz, the executive director of the Doerr Institute for New Leaders at Rice University, faced when he was a unit commander at West Point. "When you assume a leadership role, people look at you differently, and you have a status that can get in the way," and Tom makes a great point here. When we're leading others, there can be people who know *of* you but don't actually *know* you.

While Tom and his unit were in Korea, there was a soldier's wife who was pregnant. There were some complications with the pregnancy, so she got moved to a hospital in Seoul. Tom decided to call his wife and ask her to visit the soldier's wife because he thought since she was far from home and family, she would appreciate the company. The soldier kept asking Tom's wife who her husband was; when he found out, he was initially confused then realized she was talking about his unit commander. "There's a lot of power that comes from a position that has nothing to do with who I am personally," Tom said. Not many people who worked for him would have thought he cared about their personal lives.

Remember the assumptions made about you don't usually mean anything about who we truly are because they're made by people who can perceive us but don't truly know us. Rather than convincing others that we are a certain kind of individual, it's always better to simply show them through our values and heart.

When life is moving by too quickly, we can find ourselves going through the motions and becoming lost. A way to prevent this happens to be a saying that James MacIntyre, high school assistant principal and director of Mt. Adams lives by: "Don't act out of your feelings, act out of your purpose." One time James was walking through the cafeteria at the high school and saw one girl sitting by herself. He said hello as he passed by her table a few times, then one day he stopped for a conversation. It was just a simple ten-minute conversation, but he received a grateful note from the girl's mom later that day. In her note, she told James thank you because the conversation was what her daughter had needed.

For James, this instance was "such a good reminder for me. How many times I had not acted out of my purpose but acted out of my feelings and gone by...in a rush and had to get from A to B." Being aware of people around you and actively seeking out the people feeling left out is essential. This ties into the little moments in life we tend to forget because they are normal interactions for us but mean so much more to the people we interact with. James likely would have forgotten this moment if it weren't for the girl's mom taking a moment to send him a note of how much it had meant to her daughter.

There is an incredible amount of people who we interact with on a day-to-day basis. Whether this is friends or family we see or strangers we encounter while walking on the sidewalk, simply paying a little more attention in our lives can result in more intentional interactions.

When we're not paying attention, we are so focused on our own lives and living in our heads, living on autopilot. We need a small push in our day to remind ourselves of not only who we are and what we value but what actions are we willing to take to show it. This way, we also get out of our heads and back into the present world.

There is an incredible amount of people who we interact with on a day-to-day basis. Whether this is friends or family we see or strangers we encounter in an elevator or while walking on the sidewalk, simply paying a little more attention in our lives can result in more intentional interactions. When we're not paying attention, oftentimes we are so focused on our own lives and living in our heads, doing the same things we've grown accustomed to on autopilot. We need that small push in our day to remind ourselves of not only who we are and what we value but what actions are we willing to take to show that. This way, we also get out of our heads and back into the present world.

Just See

"One of the most beautiful things you can do as a human being is see the world through the lens of someone else." —Andrew Riis

In the process of touching one's heart, you may find that people have preferred ways to give and receive love. This is a concept called love languages, and Gary Chapman wrote a book on this called *The Five Love Languages: How to Express Heartfelt Commitment to Your Mate.*

The five love languages are quality time, words of affirmation, physical touch, acts of service, and gifts. People tend to have a top one or two love languages they value more than the rest. There is an online test you can take to figure out the love languages you prefer to receive.[37] Keep in mind your list can look different between what you prefer to receive and give.

Sue, previously mentioned in Chapter 2, noticed her husband doing something over the course of their marriage that relates to the love language he gives to others: acts of service. He "always sets the coffee pot at night before we go to bed so that it goes off at about five in the morning" so it's ready when she wakes up. He also would plug in her cell phone at night if she forgot so it would be fully charged in the morning. Since Sue is able to recognize her husband demonstrates his love through these acts of service, she can better acknowledge his efforts and appreciate his intentionality.

Although Gary Chapman's book focuses more on romantic relationships, love languages certainly pertain to all kinds of connections. One of the clubs I am involved in at college is the University of Washington Finance Association (UWFA), which emphasizes learning about the market and the macroeconomic trends that impact it. In 2020, after everything moved from in-person to virtual because of the coronavirus pandemic, the club officers and committee members realized UWFA was missing a social element. The Member Development Committee began hosting social hours for the club members to get to know each other in a more casual setting, and UWFA leadership had our first retreat over Zoom, which was a blend of getting to know each other and talking about how to further make UWFA flourish.

---

37   "Quizzes," *The 5 Love Languages*, accessed March 1, 2021.

After the four-hour long retreat, the committee sent out a Google Form to collect the notes from this ideation stage, but there was one addition. Under the questions for ideation, there was a place to write a note to each person on the leadership team. I had thought it would be a sweet idea to send out the notes everyone wrote to each individual. Although compiling and sending all twenty-four people their personalized PDF of notes was tedious, reading everyone's response to their notes made it worthwhile. One person's response to the notes stuck out to me—she had printed out the PDF and put it on her wall as a reminder for herself. This made me remember the impact that just a few words of affirmation can have on others and ourselves.

Life can be a rollercoaster of a journey, and it's not always an easy one. There are certain obstacles we face throughout the days, weeks, years, and more. Figuring out which love languages help remind us we are worthy, seen, and loved, keeps us going and makes our ride on the rollercoaster a bit smoother. Just like how we have our preferred ways of receiving love, so do other people around us. If we are perceptive enough, it's typically not too difficult to make an educated guess at what someone's preferred love language is to receive. If you are uncertain, you can always ask them.

Just Remember

There will be unexpected but impactful events that remind you of what's truly important. For Dakota, mentioned in the introduction, one of these moments occurred while conducting a workshop for The Young Americans, a non-profit that promotes the collective understanding and goodwill between people across the world. They cultivate this through music, dance, performance, academic education, and cultural interaction.

Dakota was in a field in Lithuania helping teach a closing number from *The Lion King*—a really emotional and powerful dance to "Circle of Life." Dakota noticed one boy crying, and he sat down with him and asked why he was sad. It turned out that the boy's entire family was in Germany, and they somehow got split up, so the boy had been spending the past few years in Lithuania in a foster home.

As everyone was listening to the music and dancing on the field, the boy told Dakota about how he used to dance with his brothers whom he hadn't seen in a few years. He told Dakota "I feel like I'm dancing with my brothers right now, and we used to dance around the house and play outside, and right now that's what we're doing...it makes me really happy, and I'm just glad to be living right now." This reminded Dakota to appreciate the small moments in life, live in the present, and not take it for granted. This is something kids tend to do better than adults; they are able to enjoy and live in the moment rather than being so fixated on the future.

Living in the present while being present with those around you is one of the best ways to develop better relationships, which is beneficial to developing the soft skills needed in life. Recognizing love languages, leveraging our knowledge of them, and practicing gratitude can help us better appreciate others in our lives, and gratitude is a foundational pillar of leadership. There are always people nearby helping, and we need to be able to support them and be grateful for them.

PART 3:

INSPIRE
YOUR LIFE

Chapter 11:
Live Your Life
Purposefully

"Life is a C between B and D. B is birth, D is death, C is choice...these difficult times can define us, these difficult times can diminish us, or these difficult times can develop us. Ultimately, we decide." —Jim Kwik[38]

What motivates you? What is your purpose? What legacy do you want to leave?

When presented with countless options for how to spend our twenty-four hours of each day, we need to have some kind of purpose that motivates us to act with purpose—how you choose to live depends on your interpretation.

Purpose

Seek discomfort.

Yes Theory is a movement of people that includes a YouTube channel with the premise of "The best things in life

---

38   Jim Kwik, "Jim Kwik - Creator Series," interview by Eric Koester, Otter.ai, September 29, 2020, audio, 38:42.

are outside of your comfort zone," as Zack Honarvar, Yes Theory's manager, describes to Jacob Kelly on *My Social Life*, a podcast centralized around social media.[39] The founders of Yes Theory, Matt, Thomas, and Ammar, create YouTube videos where they purposely put themselves out of their comfort zone and face certain fears and vulnerabilities. Zack believes Yes Theory is "a philosophy, an ideology, and a lifestyle" because they are "a movement of people that are living their lives differently than maybe [what] the status quo has laid out for them."

For the Yes Theory Family (Yes Fam), a community composed of millions around the world, following this concept of seeking discomfort can mean very different things. It could be going sky diving to face one's fear of heights or starting a conversation with a stranger every day. Maybe it's taking a cold shower, even though there's the initial two minutes of "Wow, I am freezing. This water is so cold, and I am quite uncomfortable, but I know it's helping me grow and improve my discipline," which is what Taito Okamoto, founder of the Yes Theory Japan community, tells himself each morning.

Taito told me he started a challenge where he would take a cold shower for one minute to seek discomfort. Although it was cold and took some getting used to, the one minute gradually turned into a full cold shower, and then he started to only take cold showers. Aside from helping to build Taito's self-discipline, taking these cold showers every morning serves as a reminder to live each day with purpose outside of his comfort zone.

---

39 Zack Honarvar, "Yes Theory's Manager Zack Honarvar: Why Creators Need CEOs Not Managers, the Business Side of Yes Theory," interview by Jacob Kelly, *My Social Life*, July 27, 2020, audio, 1:40:51.

A believer in early mornings, Taito's morning routine starts off with waking up at 5:45. After waking up, he will meditate and "get into the state of being grateful and humble," exercise, go to work, come back home, and train some more. At the time of our interview, Taito was training for a marathon. Since the interview, Taito has not stopped after he ran the initial marathon he was training for. He is training for a half marathon, sub-three marathon, and an Ironman. I know this sounds like an overwhelming number of uncomfortable things to do concurrently, but for Taito, it has become a habit.

After talking to Taito about his intentionality in seeking discomfort, I realized that I'd already talked to other people who seek discomfort in their own way. Barnaby Shand, founder of The Thriive Project; Yash Bhatia, podcast host of *The Mindful Youth*; Sachin Shah, podcast host of *The Sachin and Adam Show*; Andrew Riis, podcast host of *Hello, Stranger*; Stephen Edvi, the founder and director of sales at Miles Dealer; Hassan Alokaily, an engineering student at McMaster University; and Rob Lawless, a man on a mission to make ten thousand friends, are a few people in the Yes Fam who also purposefully seek discomfort in their respective lives.

Barnaby is taking a gap year to travel and explore other countries. He traveled to Italy, Spain, and Mexico and is learning the appropriate languages to communicate in each respective country.

Yash has been working on a project where he conducts FaceTime calls with one person from every state in the United States as well as one person from every country, so a total of 245 people.

Sachin traveled to Santiago, Chile by himself and "reached out to the Yes Theory community, and a guy from it took [him] hiking." Despite only knowing each other for a mere forty-eight hours, Sachin and his stranger-turned-friend decided to get a matching "YES" tattoo.

Andrew started a podcast called *Hello, Stranger* and has driven from Sydney, Australia to Cairns and back while living in a small van. This was a one-hundred-day trip spanning over six thousand miles and involving countless meaningful interactions with strangers. He truly lives by the quote, "Maybe some of the best stories are tucked away, folded into the pockets of random passers-by," which is one of the core ideas behind his podcast.

Stephen has been creating and posting four-minute YouTube videos every week. His goal is to make other people's days better through filming his and his friends' adventures. One of his videos even showed him trying chicken at the spiciest level offered.

Hassan finished his project of doing one hundred meetups with strangers where he spoke to 134 people from fifty-six different countries. For his one hundredth meetup, he invited everyone who was a part of his project to a group Zoom call and spoke about three things he had learned over his project in a TEDx Talk-like fashion.

Rob is in the midst of making ten thousand friends through talking with strangers one-on-one for one hour each and documenting his journey on Instagram under the username @robs10kfriends. He began his project in November 2015 with in-person meetups and switched to virtual meetups in March because of the pandemic. To date, he's made over four thousand friends and is working hard to meet his goal.

"Seek discomfort" is very vague, but it gives you the flexibility to choose why, what, and how you approach your goal.

"You don't need a million dollars to get out of your comfort zone." —Hassan Alokaily

When you're a leader, sometimes you have to do things beyond your level of comfort. There may be things that make you feel awkward, weird, or downright stupid. But what compels us to push through this feeling? Why do we do things outside of our comfort zone?

I remember many times in high school during lunch where, instead of sitting with my friends and talking about homework, classes, or other trivial topics, I would be in the ASB room or sitting at a table toward the end of the cafeteria trying to get students to sign up for something. Even as an ambivert, constantly asking others if they'd like to sign up for a time to donate blood for the upcoming blood drive, and mostly getting rejected, was difficult. It was awkward when I didn't know the person I was talking to and tiring because I felt obligated to maintain a smile on my face, even when I was ignored. It was not easy. But did I persist? Yes. I was not comfortable—it felt like everyone's eyes were on me. At the time, did I realize I was seeking discomfort? Maybe, but probably not. All I knew was that this was for a good cause, and someone's resounding yes outweighed the rest of the people's no.

There's one vivid memory I have from helping to recruit people for the blood drive. We had a blood droplet costume to help gain attention for the blood drive—I recall slipping it on my relatively small frame and feeling like it was Halloween, but I was dressed up in an incredibly stuffy yet baggy costume. As I walked around the cafeteria to ask random people if they would like to donate, it felt like everyone's eyes were on me again. Nevertheless, I continued approaching people. In a way, this was easier than sitting at a table because I could directly talk to people, even through the small eye holes. On the flip side, I felt completely out of my element and embarrassed, although the only thing people could see were the bottom half of my legs sticking out from under the costume.

I kept a polite smile on my face despite the flame of embarrassment. Looking back now, I learned more than I had expected to in the mere fifteen minutes. I realized some people will take me seriously in a blood droplet costume and others will not. More importantly, I discovered that despite my discomfort, momentary embarrassment was not strong enough to dissuade me from helping out a worthy cause.

Seeking discomfort doesn't have to involve wearing a costume and approaching people. It doesn't even need to include interacting with people. The point is that we all have these comfort zone bubbles. Pushing yourself and challenging yourself to do something you usually wouldn't want to do cultivates growth, especially when we are serving a purpose greater than ourselves.

Legacy

"In this world nothing can be said to be certain, except death and taxes." —Benjamin Franklin[40]

40   Madsen Pirie, "Death and Taxes," November 13, 2019.

If there's one thing we all know about ourselves, it's that we are going to die. We may not know when, where, or how, but we know it's coming at some point. Everyone dies—life is too short to not do the things you want to do. Everyone knows and understands this, but how many of us actually live this principle out?

It was a normal Sunday in St. George, Utah, except for the fact that it was raining incessantly. The weather usually resembles one similar to a desert, but every year, there is one day where it rains so hard, it floods.

Kaity Bissenden, a college student who lives in St. George, was telling me about her experience during one of these rainstorms. She was driving her car when the storm hit, and "it was the craziest rainstorm I've ever seen, and I grew up in Seattle, so I've seen some things." When her car slid off the road and into the built-in gutter to help control the floods, she tried to drive back to her apartment. However, her car got stuck in a dip of the gutter due to its low clearance. Kaity didn't know what to do and was anticipating the possibility of getting hit by another car, uncontrollable in the heavy rain.

She saw a truck drive up, and "these two guys jumped out of their truck. They pushed my car out of the gutter, and I made it home, and I never got to say a word to them because it was raining. They couldn't hear me, and I was in my car, and they jumped in the truck and drove away." She realized how what these strangers did was incredibly dangerous since they ran the risk of getting hit themselves in the low visibility.

Kaity was dumbfounded by the two strangers' intentional and selfless act since they could have driven past her and called for medical services, but they intentionally chose to risk their lives "because they genuinely cared, they were worried. They didn't even see me slide off the road; they drove up on me and were like 'Oh this girl's stuck, let's just get her out.'" This shows how unpredictable life is and serves as a reminder to live how you want to sooner rather than later because Kaity could have been seriously injured by another car.

The two men didn't care if they received recognition for their selfless act because Kaity couldn't see their faces in the heavy rain. They just cared about living out their purpose in life. You certainly don't need to risk your life to be a leader. Something to consider, though, is thinking about how you can better serve those around you. When you see a need, figuring out how you can help, and then acting on it is one of the greatest things you can do for people.

Though thinking about your own death is a little morbid, it helps you reflect on what you want your personal legacy to be. This is something that resonated with Nicole Balkenbusch, a Finance Manager at Amazon, when her husband took an MBA class about personal legacies and told her about it. She decided to write her own personal legacy and simplified it to nine purposeful words.

Nicole's personal legacy is "Strong businesswoman who helps others break down barriers." She had this painted on a canvas by a local female artist as a reminder for how she wanted to live it out. Now, the painting sits in her personal office where she can see it every day.

Each word Nicole chose has a specific meaning to her. She wants to be someone who is both mentally and physically strong and the kind of businesswoman "known for delivering results, not at any expense, but on behalf of what's needed." Because she had parents and mentors who she's been able to look to for advice, Nicole believes in lifting others with her as she climbs, even if it means it'll take longer than if she had gone by herself. The three gifts one can provide to others is time, talent, and treasure, and the final portion, "break down barriers," is Nicole's favorite expression. Whenever people tell her no, she is motivated to work even harder and determine how she can turn that no into a yes. The way her legacy is shown on the painting is through steps; they are purposefully not depicted in a straight line because she recognizes how life is not linear. Sometimes you move sideways or backwards on the journey. In the end, Nicole has something she can look to for guidance on how she wants to live her own life, but more importantly, why she wants to live that way.

"People don't buy what you do, they buy why you do it." — *Simon Sinek[41]*

Living life with intentional purpose is powerful and stems from knowing what you ultimately want in life. Having such a clear idea of your personal legacy and truly understanding what everyday leadership looks like allows you to make decisions that serve you, your goal, and others around you. The trick is figuring out a legacy authentic and true to you.

Another conversation I had about near-death experiences was with Bryant Galindo. He was at a Halloween party with his then-girlfriend and some friends in a

---

41   *TEDx Talks*, "Start with Why -- How Great Leaders Inspire Action | Simon Sinek | TedxPugetSound," September 28, 2009. Video, 18:01.

restaurant-turned-club. Everyone was wearing cos-
tumes, so it was hard to see due to the fog machines and
everybody dancing.

In the middle of dancing and out of the corner of his
eye, Bryant spotted a man not wearing a costume and
instantly got a strong, negative vibe from him. He initially thought he was just feeling protective, but when
the man came over, Bryant realized the man was trying
to stab him in the neck. Thankfully, people stepped in,
including one of Bryant's friends who ended up getting
his hand slashed by the man, so Bryant was able to leave.

Bryant was rushed to the hospital, and there were sur-
geons ready for him who said, "You know, you're lucky
to be alive. He was 0.1 centimeters away from piercing
your jugular, and you could have died instantaneously."
Everything happened so quickly for Bryant, and he was
way too close to death for comfort. Any near-death experience is terrifying, and it has the capability to strike
you to the core.

For Bryant, he didn't let it stop him from living his life as
"it became a catalyst for transforming my life. I would
not be the person I am today if it wasn't for that event...
obviously, at least afterwards, I got a little depressed"
and was asking himself "why me?" then realized "the
work was to look at that and to actually sit with the experience, and then learn."

Bryant was able to reflect on the impact of this experience and take it as a reminder of how short life is. We
don't know when or how we are going to die because we
all are vulnerable, mortal beings. Bryant was able to flip
his mindset from thinking about how short life was to

wondering how he was going to make the most of every day. This life-changing event "allows me to do the work that I do at the age that I'm doing."

Near-death experiences can severely impact our lives, which makes it even more pressing to live how we want to and with as few regrets as possible. Jesús Hijas, the author of *Unleadership: Hacia un Liderazgo más Humano en tiempos de Inteligencia Artificial*, has thought about the importance of this realization. In his book, he talks about a simple exercise where he invites his readers to sit down and write down their eulogy. This is "a way to invite people to think more transcend[ent]...because otherwise we're going to be trapped in the day-to-day." A good point Jesús brings up is that "life is defined by death...so why do you behave like you are going to be here forever?" This realization really forces you to live driven by your purpose. If we're able to start living in a way that aligns with our values and beliefs at age forty, thirty, or twenty rather than waiting until we're eighty-five years old, this makes a huge difference.

You are the author of your own life, and life is incredibly short. Each year feels like it flies by faster than the previous one. Take charge and live how you want to. Push and challenge yourself to grow and seek discomfort in the best way possible. The sooner you learn how you want to live your life, the sooner you will be able to do just that. Be yourself, know your values, and live them out. Pertaining to leadership, this same concept applies. If you don't think you can be a leader because you're not young anymore, you've grown so used to living unauthentically, and you're not being true to what you value, that's okay. It's never too late to take control of your life.

Every now and then ask yourself one question: Are you truly pushing yourself out of your comfort zone and trying to grow into a better version of yourself? It doesn't have to look like running a marathon or talking to ten thousand people around the world. Like Hassan says, seeking discomfort doesn't require one million dollars. It simply requires your energy and focus to commit to a life worth living because when you are striving toward growth, others become inspired to live in a similar fashion.

Don't just let your environment control you and your life. By controlling your environment through seeking discomfort, you control your life. Perhaps this does look like exercising more often after the countless failed New Year's resolutions or actively talking to new people to develop more friendships. But it doesn't have to.

Chapter 12:
It's the Little Things

———

"Keep showing people love because they come around."

—*Kyler Parris*

It can be tough being a leader because unless people tell you, you simply don't know what impact you're making on other people. You know what your purpose is, but is it working? You just have to keep on going and trust that it is. In these moments of doubt, remember the smallest things often mean the most. Just slow down, remind yourself what matters, and you'll receive your million-dollar paycheck.

Slow Down

When I was a junior counselor (JC) at Mt. Adams, I was asked to fetch a few extra basic supplies from the supply closet. Although it was only a ten-minute walk away from where I was, I ran over because I wanted to be as quick as possible so the delegates in my council would have the supplies sooner. It was a hot summer day, and as I ran,

I heard someone call my name. Turning around, I saw it was another JC—he stopped me, told me to close my eyes, and did a quick breathing exercise with me where we both breathed in and out in four second intervals. He told me to picture drawing a square as I breathed in, held my breath, breathed out, and held my breath. Then, he reminded me it was more than okay to take my time rather than running over and draining energy I would need later. This resonated with me, and I thanked him and continued on my way to the supply closet, walking this time. It's so easy to get caught up in all the items on your to-do list for the day and attempt to complete them as quickly as possible. This isn't inherently bad; it's just good to remind yourself to breathe once in a while so you are able to conserve energy for later.

Over the course of my book-writing journey, I had been busier than usual, which is something I anticipated— writing a book is no easy feat. In the span of two months, I had talked with over eighty people about their experiences and thoughts on leadership. I found it difficult to take breaks longer than a few minutes in between calls, so when I had a free day coming up, I purchased the ingredients for a chocolate chip cookie recipe I had been wanting to try. I made the cookie dough and popped it in the fridge to chill, planning on baking cookies the next day. Unfortunately, I was in so many back-to-back meetings that I forgot about the cookie dough, so I told myself I would bake the cookies the following day.

I had assumed the cookie dough would yield a batch of a dozen cookies, but it turned into thirty-six. Since I had such a huge surplus of cookies (not the worst problem to have), I drove to a few friends' houses to drop cookies off. After driving for an hour, I rushed home for a scheduled interview with Stephen and arrived with under five minutes to spare. I had some extra cookies since a couple friends hadn't responded to my texts yet, so I brought the plates upstairs with me and set them on my desk to deliver later.

At the beginning of the conversation with Stephen, I accidentally elbowed one of the plates and said, "Okay, I need to put these cookies somewhere else." Before we began talking about leadership, I had told Stephen about the cookies I was delivering, so my comment wasn't entirely out of context. He immediately said, "Let's have a cookie together. I'll grab an Oreo." We took a quick cookie break, which reminded me of the importance to have fun and slow down in everyday life and leadership.

When you're constantly going from place to place and getting things down, you're going to burn out. Remember leadership is also about the little things, like cookie breaks.

What Matters

"We need to be reminded more than we need to be taught."
—John Norlin

I've always been a huge fan of sticky notes and quotes. Right now, I have thirty-five sticky notes of all sizes and colors stuck to my wall next to my desk. The little tidbits of information written down range from one-word reminders to full-blown bullet pointed notes—they remind me of certain goals, inspirational quotes, and what I should keep in mind when dealing with setbacks. Being able to jot something down on a piece of paper is powerful. Just the physical act of writing helps you remember it later, and it frees your brain to focus on other pieces of information.

Leadership doesn't always have to be something big. The beauty of it usually lies in the smallest of moments and actions. What is something small that you can realistically do for others to show you care about them? That you're thinking of them? That even if you haven't talked recently, you want to know how they are doing?

Every once in a while, I'll get a "Hey, I love you!" text from one of my friends who I've known since elementary school. Although we are both busy with our lives and no longer live ten minutes away from each other, she is intentional about showing she is thinking of me. I always appreciate the text reminders.

"I'll be on Amazon, and I'll see funny little socks...and I'll just ship it to her." This is what Anna, one of my interviewees, mentioned when we were talking about ways of showing love. She likes to send gifts to her loved ones, especially when she sees something that reminds her of them. (I think it's pretty safe to assume one of Anna's primary love languages to give others is gifts.) This may be incredibly out of the blue and spontaneous, but this is one of the best things about doing these little actions for others. It doesn't take planning, so the thought and execution matter the most.

When was the last time you reminded someone you care about them? The next time you think "Oh, I should text this person and see how they're doing," don't wait. Text them immediately before you forget (I know I'm guilty of this). Actually, stop reading for a second and go text one or two people you miss and haven't talked to in a while. If you want to go the extra mile, suggest hopping on a call to catch up in the next week.

Every day, Amy Blaschka, a social media ghostwriter and Forbes Leadership Contributor, goes to Peet's Coffee for her morning latte. The morning of her husband's birthday, she asked if he wanted anything. He thought for a moment, then said he wanted to give *others* a gift. He instructed Amy to provide the barista with a loaded gift card to pay for following customers' orders until it ran out. Although no one was behind Amy when she placed her own order, the barista agreed to this arrangement.

As Amy waited for her latte, a few men entered the coffeehouse. When they discovered their coffees were on Amy's husband, they were genuinely giddy. They came over to Amy, and she told them her husband wanted her to do something nice for others on his behalf. When they asked what they could do, Amy told them, "Just do something nice for somebody else—pay it forward." Amy believes small, unexpected acts like this can make someone's day. This positivity lingers, initiating a butterfly effect and a gift that keeps on giving.

"A kind word or gesture is so simple to do, and it's remembered years later. It doesn't take much to create a lasting impact."
—Amy Blaschka

Million Dollar Paychecks

At Mt. Adams, we talked about a concept called million-dollar paychecks. This essentially represented anything worth a million bucks—not literally valued at a million dollars, of course, but more so the aha moment when you realize what you have been doing all along actually has made an impact on other people.

When Doonyah Alucozai started CoderDojoAnvil, she wanted to create a space for young kids to learn how to code based on her own passion and desire to have a similar program when she was growing up. After one of the coding sessions, a dad came up to her and asked if they could talk. Doonyah thought there was something wrong, but instead the dad said, "I just want to thank you so much for the work you're doing here," and Doonyah said it was no problem. The dad said, "You don't understand. I'm a single father, and my daughter is autistic. She doesn't have a lot of friends at school. When I bring her to your CoderDojoAnvil sessions, she feels like she has a community, and she feels like she has friends. You don't understand how rewarding that is to see as a parent." Doonyah was blown away because she didn't realize something so small for her meant so much to another person. This is when she received her own million-dollar paycheck, and she still keeps in touch with the family today.

The summer before college started, I met with a high school friend to catch up at a frozen yogurt place. It was great to reminisce about memories in our high school days, since we were official graduates. We knew we wouldn't see each other for at least a few months, so we were enjoying each other's company. When we were saying our goodbyes, she told me I had been the first friend she had made at our school, and I've had such a positive impact on her life through constantly thinking optimistically and smiling—this helped her be a better person.

I knew I had somewhat of an impact on her because we were good friends, but I never realized how much. If she hadn't told me, I probably never would have realized. I got a million-dollar paycheck just by being myself. At school I'd try to make her laugh and smile as much as possible, but that's what I try to do with most people. What I didn't realize during those moments of laughter and smiles over the last couple years is that it had drastically impacted her life.

And that's the thing, there are so many of these moments when either something clicks or someone tells you the impact you made. In his TEDx Talk, Drew Dudley calls these million-dollar paychecks "lollipop moments." This was inspired by a time during his college days when he had massively impacted another student. The girl was with her parents getting ready for registration. Self-doubt began to hit her, and "I knew I wasn't ready; I knew I had to quit." She was ready to tell her parents that they needed to leave.[42]

Just then, she saw Drew coming out of the Student Union Building holding a sign and passing out lollipops from a bucket to promote SHINERAMA, Students Fighting Cystic Fibrosis. As Drew walked down the line of people, he stopped at her. Handing a lollipop to the guy next to her, he told him, "You need to give a lollipop to the beautiful woman standing next to you." After she blushed fiercely and accepted the lollipop from the guy, Drew exclaimed to her parents, "Look at that. First day away from home, and she's taking candy from a stranger!" Everyone nearby began to laugh at Drew's joke, and it helped ease the girl's nerves. In that moment, she realized she "shouldn't quit; I knew that I was where I was supposed to be, and I knew

42   *TED-Ed*, "Everyday Leadership - Drew Dudley," August 15, 2003, video, 6:14.

that I was home." Although she and Drew haven't talked in the years since then, he left a profound mark on her life. Lollipop moments and million-dollar paychecks are essentially the same concept, just with different names.

You won't always get to hear how you've impacted people. In fact, this rarely happens, even when the impact is a large one. It's important to know *why* you're doing something because it will make everything else much more rewarding. When you do get to hear about the impact you've had, cherish these moments. Believe in yourself and the work you do. Leadership does not have simple fixes where if you do one thing, you're guaranteed a result in x number of days. It really is a lifelong journey, full of learning experiences. Just keep being the leader you are and don't forget to slow down every once in a while.

Chapter 13:
Learn How to Juggle

"You always have to remember to take care of yourself first and foremost, because when you stop taking care of yourself you get out of balance and you really forget how to take care of others." —Jada Pinkett Smith[43]

Remembering the good ol' airplane analogy is always important. If your plane is crashing, you need to put your own oxygen mask on first so this way, you can better help others with theirs. When life is feeling a tad overwhelming, make things bite sized, get organized, celebrate small wins, consider change, and remember to breathe. Leadership can be hectic, but it shouldn't always be.

Make It Bite-Sized

When faced with a seemingly insurmountable problem, what's the best way of tackling it? Generally, the first step is to analyze the task at hand and break it down

---

43   Caroline Bologna, "8 Times Jada Pinkett Smith Totally Nailed the Whole Parenting Thing," *HuffPost*, September 18, 2017.

into more digestible chunks. By doing so, it'll appear more doable—it's just like climbing a mountain. Looking at the peak from the bottom may be terrifying, but when you remember you just need to take it step by step, you realize it's no longer as impossible as you originally thought. This is the trick to most things. When you are able to think of an obstacle as little steps here and there, it makes everything much more manageable.

Anna, who was mentioned in the previous chapter, stated "As a person and as a professional, I have a lot of room to grow...the person I want to be in five years, I'm not that person, and I need to continue [taking] steps to get there." Gradual progress is still progress. No one has the same timeline as another, and there are times when we feel internal or external pressure to be at a certain place at a certain time. This could be because when we see the people around us, we're comparing ourselves to them, or maybe we just feel like we're "late" and should have already hit a certain milestone. Either way, we need to remember that while it's good to be self-aware and have a desire to improve ourselves, everyone will go through life their own way at different times.

We shouldn't try to follow someone's exact footsteps, just like how we shouldn't aim to be the same leader as someone else. The way to structure our own steps is by thinking of actionable items to make your dream a reality. This is what Anna mentioned; you need to take all your responsibilities and break them up into smaller tasks, then order them by importance.

Get Organized

Remember that "you're not going to solve it today," which is the best piece of advice Anna has received. Although you won't be able to finish everything, you can certainly solve a little part of the overall issue and continue solving more of it as you continue. If you're getting stressed out by the thought of thinking five or ten years in the future, think more short-term, like six months to a year—keep decreasing the timeframe until your task feels more attainable.

Common productivity tools include the Pomodoro technique, flowtime method, the Eisenhower matrix, to-do lists, visual schedules, or even a combination of these.

A method I use to stay organized is daily to-do lists. My list usually includes tasks that don't need to be completed by the end of the day or even week; I'm just keeping track of everything on my radar, but sometimes this backfires because I get overwhelmed from my very long to-do list. I make sure to mark the most important and urgent tasks with an asterisk—if I am able to complete the other items on my list, this is a bonus.

Another way to organize and prioritize your tasks is by using the Eisenhower matrix.[44] Once I have my complete to-do list, I draw a vertical line and a horizontal line intersecting the vertical line, creating a matrix and four quadrants. I'll go down my list, organizing them into the quadrants as I see fit. The top left quadrant should have both the urgent and important tasks, the top priority. The top right quadrant holds the important but nonurgent tasks, so second priority but tasks that often get

44 *EISENHOWER*, "The Eisenhower Matrix: How to Manage Your Tasks with Eisenhower," September 2, 2012, video, 2:24.

pushed back. For the bottom left quadrant, this has the urgent but not as important tasks, so ones to delegate to others, and the bottom right quadrant has the remaining tasks—nonurgent and not as important tasks, so these would be your lowest priority tasks.

Everyone has their own preferred method to get things done. Some people may prefer working extra hard on weekdays to have the weekends off while other people prefer distributing their work more evenly every day. What's most important is to figure out what works best for you and your style.

You can also have a specific group of people to reach out to when you need support or advice. On *My Social Life*, hosted by Jacob Kelly and previously mentioned in Chapter 11, Jacob interviews Zack Honarvar, Yes Theory's manager.[45] Zack talks about his "personal board of directors" and how he has a variety of people he checks in with on a monthly basis. This way, if Zack ever needs advice, he can hear different people's opinions.

No matter which method you opt for, or if you've chosen another one, nothing will work unless you stay disciplined. Although this is much easier said than done because humans are susceptible to distraction (including myself, very much so), by aiming for improvement every day, we will begin to see progress in our ability to get organized and stay on track.

---

45 Zack Honarvar, "Yes Theory's Manager Zack Honarvar: Why Creators Need CEOs Not Managers, the Business Side of Yes Theory," interview by Jacob Kelly, *My Social Life*, July 27, 2020, audio, 1:40:51.

Celebrate Small Wins

When Justin Nguyen graduated from the University of Central Florida in December 2018, he had a plan for what he was going to do. Although he declined a job offer with one of the Big Four accounting firms, he felt confident in choosing to work on *Declassified College*. While focusing on producing content for the podcast, it wasn't until six months later when Justin realized his internship money was becoming depleted. Since *Declassified College* wasn't bringing in steady income, he needed to start making money again to pay bills, so he began doing some LinkedIn consulting.

A few months later, Justin was feeling burnt out. He'd been working incredibly hard on his LinkedIn content, but "even though [he] was growing and revenue was coming in, [he] wasn't celebrating it." Then, in October 2019, Justin was invited to speak in Dubai about LinkedIn, which was a pivotal and validating moment—it was finally a big win he felt like he could celebrate. Since then, *Declassified College* has continued to grow, and Justin realizes he "should have actually celebrated [him] winning that contract for [LinkedIn] because that helped [him] get here, that helped [him] build a reputation to get here, that grew the podcast." Now he ensures to celebrate both the large wins and the smaller ones that helped him get there.

When we're constantly working and working and working on what we're trying to accomplish, the little tasks we finish day-to-day can feel minimal and unworthy of a celebration. And maybe they aren't, but this doesn't mean you shouldn't appreciate, recognize, and value yourself for finishing them. Even when your progress feels slow, big wins take time—it's all a part of the process.

Change Can Be Good

Life is hard, and when we are trying and failing to juggle everything, it may be best to just change our situation.

When we have been participating in an activity for a long time, it tends to be a part of our identity. For Snehaa Ganesh Kumar, this activity was spelling bee competitions. She competed in her first spelling bee as a kindergartener—after realizing she was good at spelling words, she continued to compete at regional and national competitions. Although she loved the challenge of spelling hard words, Snehaa realized some changes were needed. The emphasis on the competition was so high that there was no concern for the competitors' mental health and "people judge[d] you 100 percent based on your ranking." Snehaa felt obligated to include her ranking when introducing herself to others because of this.

When you're competing in spelling bees, various factors affect your performance, and they're not all controllable. How you perform is a "product of the specific words that you [got] in a day." Snehaa would often feel frustrated because she thought if she had received another person's word, she could have performed better. Now, Snehaa is trying to shift the innate competitive pressure in spelling bees through a podcast where she interviews competitors about their experiences. She hopes this will show how there's more to spelling bees than what you see on TV.

Snehaa was able to recognize how toxic the spelling bee environment was for her—it bred competitiveness beyond a reasonable degree—and initiate change. While it is tough to weigh the inherent uncertainty that comes with change, especially when we are so accustomed to our environment being one way, leaders need to be the catalyst.

Amy, who was mentioned in the previous chapter, had to deal with change when she transitioned from being an organizational consultant to a writer. It was tough for her initially because she "made the mistake of trying to be all things to all people...'writer' is a general term that covers a lot of ground." After she pivoted careers, she was concerned about niching down, fearing it would mean losing out on potential projects (and income) and didn't want to limit herself.

However, accepting every writing assignment meant she was spreading herself thin and working on pieces she didn't love. She realized "just because you can do something doesn't mean you should," and focused on putting her talents to their best use. Amy promoted her specific writing niche to attract and accept opportunities that were a good fit—doing so made it easier for her ideal clients to find her and for Amy to do more of the work she loved.

Figuring out what is best for you is not easy. It's usually much easier to figure out what you don't like and cross it off. Although you can't always change your situation, you usually have two options. If you don't like your situation, try to change it. If you are unable to, then you either have to change your mindset or accept your situation for what it is.

Just Breathe

What Matthew Henry, author of *Working Together: Why We Need Bipartisanship in American Politics* and *Dating Yourself: Finding Self-Love Before True Love*, learned through writing his two books is how important properly communicating with others is. This means "not saying yes just to say yes. It's okay to say no and to go against the grain because by doing so, that's how your voice is amplified...If you say yes to everything, you're actually doing a disservice to both yourself and your team." If you disagree with something, say so. Communicating your actual opinion rather than saying something to please others will make you much happier. Don't succumb to groupthink because "real leadership is about making those tough decisions. It's saying what no one else is saying."

While saying no, it's also important to remember that "every time you say no to something, you are simultaneously saying yes to something else."[46]

"You can't give 100 percent of you if you don't take care of yourself first." —Leander Howard II

One week during my sophomore year in college, I was overextended and unnecessarily stressed out—I had been planning a four-hour long club retreat, I was worried about my classes, and I cared too much about what other people thought of me. I wasn't prioritizing my health, time, or emotions. I typically have a strong handle on my stress

---

46   Pamela Mendelsohn, "The Importance of Saying 'No,'" *MyTherapyNYC*, July 26, 2019.

level and am able to prevent my hypothetical boat from getting rocked—this week was different.

Although I wanted to be productive that night, I decided to call a friend and talk. Right when the call connected, the dam holding back my emotions broke, and I started crying. We spoke for an hour over the phone, and I just poured my thoughts and feelings out to him. This was a much-needed, cathartic cry because I had been feeling so terribly about myself. Talking out loud was helpful in organizing my thoughts and giving me some semblance of my usual logical mind—I finally got everything off my chest after having repressed it for so long. Hearing his opinion and advice was also helpful because when you're stuck in the cycle of overthinking, it's tough to see the big picture. He reminded me that the only person I could control in life was myself, and no matter how much I tried, there was nothing I could do about how people perceived me, what people thought, and how people acted. There are countless things in life that we have absolutely no control over, and other people is one of them. This was the reminder I needed to regain control of my thoughts and emotions.

Preventing stress is much easier than reducing it, and two of my favorite tips to stay internally balanced are to talk with someone and do a brain dump. When I talk to people, often in the form of an impromptu FaceTime video call, it's helpful to talk about how I'm feeling and what's been on my mind. Asking how the other person has been doing is also recommended because this way, you can focus on someone else. Perhaps you've been too zoomed in or out when thinking about everything you need to get done, so you can adjust and see everything in perspective.

Another tip is following the process of a brain dump, a technique that Mel Robbins, a TV host, author, and motivational speaker, promotes. It entails taking a pen and paper and writing down everything on your mind. This can be a task you've been procrastinating on, an important errand you need to run, or anything on your mind or to-do list. Once you have finished, highlight the top three things you believe are most important and do them.[47] This will help you clear your mind (by writing everything that's been on your mind) and set your priorities for the day (the top three things you need to do). You'll feel refreshed and productive, hopefully with a new perspective ready to tackle the rest of the day.

When you're staying productive and getting things done, remember to set boundaries for yourself. You need to prioritize *yourself* and remember your limits. If you continuously overexert yourself, then you'll burn out sooner. Think of yourself as a candle. If you burn one for more than four hours at a time, carbon will collect on the wick and make it unstable, resulting in a smoking candle. On the other hand, if you burn it in shorter intervals, you'll burn better and more evenly.

Taking mental breaks regardless of whether you're working individually or in a team is necessary because expecting 100 percent effort from ourselves 100 percent of the time is not sustainable. We are humans, not productivity robots.

There won't always be a clear blue sky—you will get busy and stressed out, but it's crucial to remember you got

47   *Mel Robbins*, "How to Stop Feeling Overwhelmed Right Now | Mel Robbins," August 13, 2018, video, 3:42.

this. Just like there are highs and lows in life, leadership isn't always a straight trajectory. There will be unexpected speed bumps where you need to take it slow so you don't wreck your car, or long, empty strips where you are able to accelerate your speed. We have twenty-four hours in each day—whether your day has been one of the best or one of the worst, it'll only last for this specified amount of time. Enjoy the best days in life to the fullest and remember that the worst days always end. There will always be a discrepancy between everything we want to accomplish and what we can realistically handle, but prioritize yourself. Take everything step by step, get organized and recalibrate your priorities, celebrate the small wins, change and adjust if needed, and breathe. Remembering what you can and can't control in life is the key to staying balanced as a leader.

Chapter 14:
Lead Yourself

"We are responsible for our own lives." —Stephen Covey[48]

This is your life. It's not your parents' life, your friend's life, or a stranger's life. It's yours. Only you can choose what you do and don't do. When you make decisions on leading yourself, remember to take action, be yourself, and live by your values.

Just Do It

When Carina Musolino, entrepreneur and founder of 5th & Venus, dropped out of college when she was twenty-one years old to join the startup world, she didn't know where life would take her. In the startup world, you're "thrown to the wolves...you own your department, and you have to figure it out." Although initially this was a tough adjustment, she grew a lot from needing to be her own leader. She was learning from various people

---

48 J.D. Meier, "The Best Stephen Covey Quotes That Will Empower You," *Sources of Insight.*

and didn't always have the best role models to look to for guidance, but this journey has led her to where she is now. She believes people should be leaders early on rather than only stepping back and observing—when you lead, you can pick up more attributes of other leaders around you.

What Carina wished she had known before is you can "accept everyone's perspective, but that doesn't mean you need to be attached to it." Carina had picked up negative attributes she needed to work on and adjust. Countless people will give you their advice on what to do, and this can be helpful, but think about what resonates with *you* the most. One technique or habit won't work for everyone, so it's important to understand who you are and where you want to be. Carina asks herself a question before taking action: "Do these actions resonate with me and fuel the leader I want to become?"

Once you understand what you want to do, you can take action. Edozie Ezeanolue, a student at the University of Notre Dame and the founder and CEO of NXSTEP Co., realized his passion for entrepreneurship and creation in middle school. He officially acted on this interest in high school when he started a clothing charity business and a shoe business. His clothing charity business was South BeND Apparel where he designed and sold shirts—the profits were donated to Center for the Homeless in South Bend, and he would purchase shoes in high demand and sell them for his shoe business. After building the foundation for his two businesses, Edozie is now working on NXSTEP Co., a platform that connects high school students with current college students. Edozie was inspired to start this initiative because when he was applying to colleges, he wasn't able to visit and tour colleges, so he wanted to help bridge this accessibility gap for other students.

As a role model to his younger siblings, Edozie is aware of how much of an impact he has on those around him, even when he doesn't realize it. While working on his businesses, Edozie's younger siblings took notice, especially his nine-year-old brother. He's always asking, "What are you doing...what's this business now...how's this going?" One day, he told Edozie he wanted to start a business like him, and this drives Edozie to work even harder on NXSTEP and turn it into something his younger brother will be inspired by.

How often do you find yourself looking back with regret? Maybe you would love to travel the world more and wish you had taken that opportunity to visit Singapore. Or maybe it isn't traveling for you. Maybe you were debating between learning Spanish and Italian and ended up not learning either language. This can be anything you've been wanting to do but are finding yourself stuck in taking that first step. Don't wait, just go for it.

One thing Erinn, previously mentioned in Chapter 4, believes is that when you are the captain of your own ship, "you own your attitude, you own your choices, you own your decisions...once people take accountability for those decisions and those choices, it can be so freeing and empowering." Being able to steer your own ship in whichever direction your heart desires is pivotal, and Erinn underscores the importance of not only making *your* decision but also making *a* decision. One of her favorite quotes is "Indecision is a decision" because she's grown used to seeing people who go back and forth on their decisions. Rather than going with one and sticking with it, she notices people get paralyzed or are looking for the perfect option when in reality, there usually is no perfect option. Aiming for progress rather than perfection is so much more important. This way, no matter where you start, you can keep moving forward. Even when things take a turn for the worst, you are able to continue despite the obstacles you face.

This is also something Ben Fields, a PhD student at the University of California, Berkeley, realized. When he was an undergraduate student at Cornell University, he was "on a quest to be the best that [he could] possible be." For him, this meant taking advantage of all the opportunities, the academic ones in particular, Cornell offered. Once he created a game plan for what he wanted to do, he executed it. Ben graduated with a double major in global and public health sciences and development sociology as well as an octuple minor in inequality studies—health equity track, demography, international development studies, public service studies, science communication and public engagement, biological sciences, environment and sustainability, and law and society.

Although Ben had a clear idea of what he wanted to do and how to get there, you might not know where you want to lead yourself. If you don't know what you're interested in or passionate about, exploration is key. Remember who you are and what you value.

Just Be You

"I can have influence, and I can have an impact on others... without having any title, and I didn't have to be this super

accomplished person to make somebody have a better day than they were having." —Rayna LaFave-Clark

You don't need a position or a title to impact people and be a leader. Sure, it is easier to inspire more people when you have a large following, but it is not a necessity. It doesn't really matter too much where you start. It's all about where you end up.

Barnaby, previously mentioned in Chapters 7 and 11, realized something as he was growing older. He noticed that "over the years, it's almost as if I've just been watching my community self-destruct on every level, mentally...few people have come through these teenage years unscathed." There were numerous teens he knew directly or indirectly going through challenges with their mental health. Witnessing this "imbued me with this sense of responsibility," and Barnaby thought that if he didn't share his own challenges and experiences, then who would?

"However unnatural it is for me to kind of put myself out there, be uncomfortable, attempt to be a leader and impact people, I've got to do it," Barnaby said. He believed that if he didn't share his story because of a lack of courage, he would be doing a disservice to not only himself but also to those around him. Barnaby has taken the first step to do what resonated with him, and no matter where it takes him, I think it says a lot about who he is.

One method Mark Metry, podcast host of *Humans 2.0* and author of *Screw Being Shy*, uses to live the life he wants is daily meditation. What Mark has learned is that "anybody can read a book. Anybody can listen to a podcast. But not everyone actually understands...they don't actively try to integrate it in their own life." To Mark, meditation is one of the few activities that helps bridge the gap between kind of knowing something and actually understanding it because you're only focusing on one thing for an extended period of time.

Through meditation, Mark has taught his brain various triggers, one being called the doorway trigger, where whenever he is about to walk through a doorway, he takes a deep breath and smiles. Another trigger is whenever he feels anxiety creeping in, he will immediately know to stop what he's doing and go outside for a walk rather than pushing through the anxiety. If Mark's brain begins to create potential stories based on a small piece of information, like where "this person said this thing to me, do they hate me...and that could be truthful, or it could be completely false." Whenever he believes his brain is trying to tell him false information, he asks himself "Is that really true? Who told me that?"

He credits meditation for being the tool that has helped him lead the way he lives his life and would recommend it to other people. This is because "meditation is one of the very few moments in your life where you are going to disconnect from your external environment." You're able to clear your mind, focus on the present moment and your breath, and think about what truly makes you happy without life's common stressors diverting your attention.

Whenever I ask others about an activity they're involved in and genuinely enjoy doing, they often respond with, "What you give is what you get." What you put into life is what you get out of it. Take initiative, and start doing if you have a clear vision.

Just Remember Your Values

As you're taking all these first steps in life, remember what you value. If you value being honest, speak your truth. If you value being ethical, look into ways to do this every day. If you value giving back, find non-profits that focus on what you are passionate about.

After Eddie Cosgrove, co-founder of Pogo Eclipse, graduated from college, he "interviewed all over the place for some good jobs with some very big companies…I found myself trying to adapt to the role that they were trying to peg me in and being a fake person and trying to just fit the bill because I needed a job." Eddie was in a final round interview with Amazon, but the interview didn't go as planned—it made them reconsider everything. He was tired of going after a job in something that he simply was not passionate about, so he decided to pivot and go back to school. Eddie believes sometimes we're so keen on adapting to tough situations that we just look for short-term rewards and choosing immediate success over putting in the work for more long-lasting success. Really homing in and putting in the efforts result in more long-term success. Now, Eddie is working at a company he built and believes in, and one where he is excited to work at.

This is something that Aaryan Shah, a university student at Macquarie University, realized. He looks up to tri-athlete, rower, and motivational speaker John Maclean. When John was about twenty-two years old, he became a paraplegic when he was hit by a truck and injured his spine. Despite this obvious hurdle in his life, John went on to compete in triathlons and worked incredibly hard to be able to relearn how to walk.[49]

The reason why Aaryan looks up to John is because of his mindset. John continues to push himself forward, not because he has to but because he wants to. This especially resonates with Aaryan because they have both endured rehabilitation to be able to walk. John does a great job of looking ahead and "doesn't see anything as a setback...he is constantly working toward something bigger and better than what he is now." Through persevering no matter what the challenges, John has inspired countless people to lead themselves, and this certainly includes Aaryan.

One way Aaryan has led himself is through raising $750,000 for a fundraising event for the Cerebral Palsy Alliance by climbing Mount Kosciuszko. With the help of a law firm sponsoring him, Aaryan was able to give back to the organization that had given so much to him. Being able to see the direct impact he was making by climbing the mountain was also a source of motivation. Aaryan knows that "if it's something you're passionate about, you will do everything you can to reduce the injustice," and if it isn't something that matters to you, then you're not going to do as much about it.

When you are leading yourself and a team around you, it's immensely important to also get to know the people on your team and ask for feedback on how you are doing. This furthers the trust between you and each individual on your team. They know you are serious

---

49   Lizza Gebilagin, "Reach Your Potential: Life Lessons from John Maclean Who Learned to Walk Again," *The Daily Telegraph,* January 15, 2017.

about listening and enacting change. This is what Kyler Parris, a university student at Occidental College, made sure to do when he was a campaign manager. Kyler is someone who "want[s] to work with people that are going to be powered by passion for the issues [they're] fighting for," rather than people who are solely driven by an ulterior motive, like receiving a letter of recommendation. Although it was difficult for him to get to know everyone on his team of eighteen interns, especially since they were all virtual, he was intentional about building these personal connections through socially distanced outdoor gatherings and creating an inclusive and supportive zoom culture.

Kyler wanted to be proactive about asking for feedback from his team. After the first few weeks of the internship, he sent a survey asking for qualitative and quantitative data for how the internship program had been thus far. This included questions on how the interns felt about the impact they were making, if they felt valued, their workload, and suggestions for how the internship program could be improved. One piece of feedback he received was that the interns wanted more notice about new projects and opportunities, and Kyler made sure to improve this. Overall, it "felt really rewarding to see these people say that they felt valued," despite all the relationships being built virtually. It showed him how through leading himself and his team, he was still able to establish a community, a characteristic necessary in leadership.

After a few years of living and reflecting as a monk, Matt Tenney, CEO of The Generous Group and TEDx Talk speaker, understood what he wanted to do. His mission was to serve and love others, so he kept looking for different ways to do this. Matt has co-founded and led several non-profit organizations, and he realized that regardless of the type of business, teaching leaders to love their people was foundational to success, both in and outside of financial success. Through this realization, he decided to start his non-profit because he wanted to impact more people's lives by inspiring the leaders of the companies. The idea of impact has led his life in various directions.

One thing Matt points out when leading yourself is "if you're just comfortable enough and you have just enough things to distract yourself, then you won't ever start asking the real difficult question, which is 'What's a life truly worth living?'" To him, the answer is simple:

- Are you happy?

- Are you kind to others?

Although it comes down to only two questions, Matt recognizes how this is not easy to do. Nevertheless, all we can do is keep trying and do our best.

The way Michael Larson, a college student at Gonzaga University with a leadership minor, realized his passion goes back to when he attended Mt. Adams, the same leadership camp I went to. There, he realized he simply wanted to serve people, love people, and through this, make a difference in the world. Mt. Adams helped spark the "desire and fire within me to want to do something to make the world a better place. I didn't know what it was going to be at the time, but I knew that." Michael no longer wanted to be an aerospace engineer and design planes for a living—he wanted to impact people's lives more directly.

After Michael ran for ASB in high school and was elected, he had an idea to serve the students. He conferred with his leadership teacher and ASB advisor, Mrs. Waller, and told her his idea. This was Ice Cream and Compliments, where students would get free ice cream from leadership students during lunch by writing a compliment for another person. Through this, Michael's idea would hit three of the five love languages (acts of service, gifts, and words of affirmation), and he believed it would be a powerful thing to do every Friday. Mrs. Waller then responded with, "Michael, why'd you even ask me? Why don't you just go do it? You already know what to do, you don't need me, just go do it." This encouragement enabled Michael to realize how he could take his ideas and actually make them happen.

"If my ideas were like the wood to a fire, then Mrs. Waller's encouragement was a spark and the lighter fluid that caught everything else on fire," said Michael.

Since then, Michael has been applying this idea of "You already know how to do it. Just go do it," to other projects he has worked on, like Meals in the Margins, a project that serves the homeless population in Spokane, Washington. Students will provide meals to people in need, and they'll sit down with them and have a conversation. Michael is not only helping to feed those who need it the most, but he's also humanizing them. Homeless people often get poorly treated just because they don't have a consistent place to stay. We all go through tough times in life, so it's important to remember we are all much more alike than we are different.

The best kind of experience you can get is firsthand experience, and there aren't very many things in the world that you will fully understand just from passively learning about it. You have to try new things, make mistakes, learn from them, and let them guide you through in the future. Step number one for doing anything is simply taking action and remember you have impact just by being yourself.

Leading yourself looks different for everyone. There are no prerequisites to leadership and remember how all setbacks teach you something, whether it's about yourself or others. Lead yourself in the direction that is best for you and others will begin to take notice. You truly do miss 100 percent of the shots you don't take. Sometimes you are aiming in the wrong direction or your hand falters at the last second, but you'll always be eagerly watching the ball leave your hands to see where it ends up landing.

Chapter 15:
Reminders

———

"Stories are powerful because they transport us into other people's worlds but, in doing that, they change the way our brains work and potentially change our brain chemistry—and that's what it means to be a social creature." —Paul Zak[50]

I hope you understand why I chose to include so many stories. Maybe there were stories that made you want to push yourself out of your comfort zone, stories that touched your heart, and stories that prompted you reflect to on how you can be an even better leader moving forward.

Nothing will change unless you do. Whether this is your mindset, your actions, or what you tell yourself, in order to create change in your life, it all begins with you. Take these stories with you, and live life more intentionally aware of your influence and potential to inspire yourself and others.

———

50   Elizabeth Robinson, "Storytelling versus Storymaking," *Max Influence* (blog), *MtoM Consulting*, November 17, 2014.

As you know, leadership isn't constrained to one aspect of your life or limited to people with titles and power. There are no prerequisites because leadership is bigger than that. Leadership is about life as a whole.

This book was originally going to be about the intersection of leadership and youth, but things changed; as I continued speaking to more and more people who were established professionals rather than students or young adults, I realized I didn't want to limit this book. Leadership is ageless, and there is always room to grow and develop in your own journey.

We truly are all just humans on Earth trying to human together. The journey from x to y is one that is uncertain, but it's part of what keeps life so exciting. Change is one of the few guarantees in life.

Shower Thoughts

When you realize something life-changing, it's typically while you are caught off guard in the dullest moments of what life has to offer. Taking a shower is considered a pretty mundane task, and oftentimes I find myself going through the motions on autopilot and listening to music at full blast to block out my thoughts. On one Friday night, I found myself changing up my routine a smidge.

A friend told me how he had taken a shower in the dark, apart from a small night light, at two in the morning. As he described how much he enjoyed the experience and would suggest it to others, I was thinking about how I would be terrified to do just that. Despite this, I told him I would try it out sometime.

After this, I was in a meeting with my group members for a class project and a client we were working with. At the end of the meeting, the client mentioned something that resonated with me: Throughout various milestones in her life, she believed she would be really smart, accomplish great things, and have her life figured out. However, it didn't end up being the case. She realized that although she was bright and accomplished, she still didn't have her life figured out. This is when she realized everyone, not just her, was making up things as they go and people who appeared to always have their life figured out were simply better at faking it.

Later that day, I found myself in a Women in Finance meeting where we discussed impostor syndrome and its effects on how women view themselves as inferior to men, even when they have more experience. It was an open conversation and a safe space to voice our opinions and stories. Once the meeting ended and everyone left, my friend Ahlam, previously mentioned in Chapter 4, and I stayed to catch up and check in on each other.

We talked more about impostor syndrome and how much fear can impact us negatively. Ahlam oftentimes finds herself stuck because although she wants to try new things, she's scared of initiating something at the risk of appearing unintelligent. I admire Ahlam and am constantly amazed by her unique ability to be a constant joy in other people's lives and include everyone, but she doesn't see how this equates to her having value. This frustrates me since her strengths are ones that cannot be taught, and I find emotional intelligence and internal enthusiasm so much more valuable than the ability to memorize and regurgitate information on an exam.

Dealing with impostor syndrome is incredibly difficult; no matter where you are and what you are doing, no one will be able to change your mind. What someone tells you can only shift your perspective for so long. Only you are truly capable of believing in yourself; other people can help you bolster your self-confidence, but it is a temporary change.

I told Ahlam what my client had told me earlier that day: Everyone is simply making up things as they go, and no one has their life together all the time. And this is okay. We're always learning from our experiences, and it's not expected of us to understand everything right off the bat. Sometimes we need to push ourselves out of our comfort zone and try new things because it's when we witness the most growth in ourselves.

After our nearly three-hour-long conversation, I was left to ponder and reflect on what we had discussed. I decided to follow my initial friend's suggestion and take a shower at night and purposely turn the light off before hopping in. Although the idea worried me, I wanted to push myself out of my comfort zone and try something new.

It took some time for my eyes to adjust to the darkness that suddenly enveloped me, but I was committed. I relished living in the moment and taking a leap of faith despite my fear. Being brave doesn't require the lack of fear but rather the commitment to doing something despite being scared; it doesn't have to require a huge step, either. The longer the lights were off, the more I realized my friend was right—I was able to be at peace and think clearly for the first time in a while. There were no distractions and there was a magical ambiance. I relished it. Of course, not all new experiences will be positive, but putting yourself out of your comfort zone and saying yes to growth and life is worthwhile.

I genuinely hope this book and the countless stories within have resonated with you. This has transformed into a passion project, a difficult yet rewarding challenge, and a reason to reach out to others, both strangers and longtime friends.

Regardless of where you are and who you are, I want you to remember something. If there's one thing that you take away from this book, please let it be this: You are capable of so much more than you think, and you are enough just the way you are. Start from within and let your mindset and perspective guide you, and remember to look at life in a different light (or without any light) every once in a while. Life is an assortment of random experiences and memories, but that's one of the beautiful aspects about it.

Go out there and change the world, person by person. How, you might ask? By starting with yourself and simply being you.

Resources

Chapter 6

What helped Akash Karia improve his presentation skills the most was recording his speeches. Every time he gave a speech, he used a video camera to record it; then, he would review it and look for certain patterns and mannerisms he wanted to change.

Chapter 13

Pomodoro technique:

1. Create a list of tasks.
2. Set a timer for twenty-five minutes and work on your tasks until the time runs out.
3. When the twenty-five minutes is over, take a five-minute break.
4. Repeat steps two and three two more times.
5. Take a fifteen-minute break instead of your regular five-minute break.

Congratulations, you've just finished one cycle! A common variation is working in fifty-minute intervals and then taking ten-minute breaks and a half hour to substitute the fifteen-minute one.

Flowtime method:

This is similar to the Pomodoro technique, but the structure emphasizes mood rather than time. If you lean away from strict schedules that outlay exactly what you have to do and for how long, then this is for you. Instead of working in twenty-five-minute intervals and taking periodic breaks, you work for however long you want to and take breaks as needed.

I prefer this method over the Pomodoro technique most days because when I have meetings throughout the day, it helps me have an idea of which tasks I need to accomplish by when to stay on track.

Eisenhower matrix:

This is detailed in Chapter 13.

To-do list:

Write down a complete list of everything you need to accomplish. This is similar to Mel Robbin's brain dump, detailed in Chapter 13.

For my especially time-crunched days, I will create a to-do list and then organize them into the Eisenhower matrix to get a better sense of which tasks are most important and urgent; then, I can prioritize completing those.

Visual schedule:

There are various tools to help you create a visual depiction of events on your schedule. My personal favorite is

Google Calendar, and I actually started using it because I was scheduling interviews for the book. Now, I put down all my meetings, events, and other important items on my calendar. I also color code everything, so meetings for one club will be a different color than my class schedule. You can also use visual schedules for time blocking, which is when you add a time on your calendar dedicated to completing a certain task.

It's up to your discretion as to how much or little you use these tools. I'm sure there are plenty of other ones available, such as the Kanban board, but these are the ones I personally have tried and still use.

Acknowledgments

I never thought I'd be a published author. After all, I've always been more of a reader, and after years of reading in the car, this is why I need a GPS to navigate half the time I drive. Although this journey has challenged me and is both the easiest and hardest thing I've ever done, I'm so glad I had taken that first step on this journey. It's taught me so much about myself, other people, and how comfortable it is typing on my bed rather than at my desk, given the number of times I fell asleep writing.

All jokes aside, the biggest takeaway writing *Bigger Than Leadership* is that publishing a book takes a village. I am endlessly grateful to everyone for all the support. This book would not be here without you.

Thank you to my family for everything even though I forgot to tell you about this book until two months in.

Thank you to my friends for checking in and always providing me with encouragement.

Thank you to my beta readers and editors. This book would be 10,000 words longer and full of fluff (aka not good) without you all.

Thank you to my interviewees, both named and anonymous. Keep sharing your stories.

Thank you to my readers. Even if I don't know you, I appreciate you for taking the time to read this book and my Acknowledgments page.

Last but not least, thank you to everyone who took a risk on me and pre-ordered my book. This book would not be here without your support, and I appreciate you all.

Jesús Hijas Carretero	Jennifer Macaulay
Larry Shan	Candy Cook
YuYu Madigan	Gary Cook
Boh Dickey	Melleny Cook
Janet Lopez	Weili Ge
Erin Molay	Audra O'Neil
Eric Koester	Michael Bunch
Taryn Lum	Alexa Smith
Dimitri Yang	Richie Duangmani
Alfred Mugho	Aijana Zellner
Lauren Macey	Patricia Li
John Norlin	Minami Wakabayashi
Lauren Johnson	Rick McPherson
Hannah Bellinger	Michelle Lee
Simon Parsons	Mikee Cagampan
Christina Nichols	Kendrick Lu
Phillip Quinn	Doug Hakala
Houston Kraft	Ben Fields
Andre Samandari	Tonya Shum
Michael Albrecht	Victoria Brodsky
Kaity Bissenden	Megan McIntyre
Ryan Fehr	A.J. Hostak

Akash Karia
Laura Edwards
Tom Lee
Andrea Pesola
Ricki Pasinelli
Debbie Brooks
Sidney Danielle
Simran Sall
Coonoor Behal
Mozes Jacobs
Frank Hodge
Amberine Wilson
Darci Curtin
Raveena Nair
Theresa Shek
Michael Chung
Chloe Chung
Jack Whelan
Elena Baraznenok
Alexandria Zamora
Scott Bertram
Jon Bahr
Frances Maloy
Meridith Fishkin
Allison Eng
Kelly Haupt
Carlos Lazo
Idolka Cruz Bao
Amy Blaschka
Khoi Nguyen

Claire Farr
Michael Catanese
Ivette Gomez
Kirk Johnson
Rick Ferrell
Arun Solanky
Gabriela Michan
Jenny Gawronski
Kristina Te
Kurt O'Brien
Nadia Delgado Reina
Robi Lin
Kevin Garcia
Frank Huang
John Zagula
Andrew Riis
Janelle Acevedo
Daisy Bugarin
Sheila Guard
Riley Messinger
Jenessa Cordero
Hanh Do
Teresa Jensen
Rebekah Bastian
Tiffany Wong
Megan Wong
Nicole Balkenbusch
Nam Justin Lam
Ismail Abdullah
William Toycen Weyerhaeuser

Meg Collver

Morgan Hartman

Justin Camputaro

Emma Branch

Grace Deng

Amrit Singh

Orrin Harbol

Kyler Parris

Appendix

Introduction

Ariel Group (blog). "Why Storytelling Works: The Science." December 26, 2020. https://www.arielgroup.com/why-storytelling-works-the-science/.

Maxwell, John C. *The 21 Irrefutable Laws of Leadership: Follow Them and People Will Follow You.* Nashville: HarperCollins Leadership, 1998.

TEDx Talks. "Great leadership comes down to only two rules | Peter Anderton | TEDxDerby." TEDx Talks. July 25, 2016. Video, 17:29. https://www.youtube.com/watch?v=oDsM-lmfLjd4.

Chapter 1: Leadership

Boogaard, Kat. "What Kind of Leader Are You? 8 Common Leadership Styles (and Their Pros and Cons)." *Getting Ahead. The Muse.* Accessed March 1, 2021. https://www.themuse.com/advice/common-leadership-styles-with-pros-and-cons.

DreamLife News (blog). "Robert Downey Jr.'s Heroic Recovery: From Addict To Iron Man." June 26, 2020. Accessed January 10, 2021. https://dreamliferecovery.com/robert-downey-jr-s-heroic-recovery-from-addict-to-iron-man/.

King, Albert S. "Evolution of Leadership Theory." *SAGE Publications* 15, no. 2 (April 1990): 43-56.

TEDx Talks. "Great leadership comes down to only two rules | Peter Anderton | TEDxDerby." July 25, 2016. Video, 17:29. https://www.youtube.com/watch?v=oDsMlmfLjd4.

Chapter 2: Act on Your H.E.A.R.T.

Goleman, Daniel and Richard E. Boyatzis. "Emotional Intelligence Has 12 Elements. Which Do You Need to Work On?" Harvard Business Review, February 6, 2017. https://hbr.org/2017/02/emotional-intelligence-has-12-elements-which-do-you-need-to-work-on.

TEDx Talks. "Why the Best Leaders Make Love the Top Priority | Matt Tenney | TedxWestchester." TEDx Talks. December 5, 2019. Video, 9:52. https://www.youtube.com/watch?v=qCVoohdyI6I.

White, Sarah K. "What Is Transformational Leadership? A Model for Motivating Innovation." *CIO,* February 21, 2018. https://www.cio.com/article/3257184/what-is-transformational-leadership-a-model-for-motivating-innovation.html.

Chapter 4: Intentionality

Russell, Joyce E. A. "Career Coach: The Power of Using a Name." *The Washington Post*, January 12, 2014. https://www.

washingtonpost.com/business/capitalbusiness/career-coach-the-power-of-using-a-name/2014/01/10/8ca03da0-787e-11e3-8963-b4b654bcc9b2_story.html.

Tilokani, Devesh. "Ep 097 - Is Listening More Important Than Talking?" November 4, 2020. In *Progressholic*. Produced by Devesh Tilokani. Podcast, 10:06. https://www.progressholic.com/podcast/episode/fd46769d/ep-097-is-listening-more-important-than-talking.

Chapter 5: Better Together

Gaskell, Adi. "New Study Finds That Collaboration Drives Workplace Performance." *Forbes.* June 22, 2017. https://www.forbes.com/sites/adigaskell/2017/06/22/new-study-finds-that-collaboration-drives-workplace-performance/?sh=62dc668d3d02.

Growth, Aimee. "You're the Average of the Five People You Spend the Most Time With." *Business Insider,* July 24, 2014. https://www.businessinsider.com/jim-rohn-youre-the-average-of-the-five-people-you-spend-the-most-time-with-2012-7.

Hollday, Anne E. "Relationships and Social Connections Can Help You Live Longer." *Health and Wellness* (blog), *UPMC*, January 22, 2019. https://www.susquehannahealth.org/in-the-community/blog/relationships-and-social-connections-can-help-you-live-longer.

Hope, Miranda." One Friend | Miranda Hope | TEDxCharlottesville." TEDx Talks. Posted on February 7, 2020. YouTube video, https://www.youtube.com/watch?v=hTdWA-V1WGQ.

Mineo, Liz. "Good Genes Are Nice, but Joy Is Better." *Harvard Gazette*, April 11, 2017. https://news.harvard.edu/gazette/story/2017/04/over-nearly-80-years-harvard-study-has-been-showing-how-to-live-a-healthy-and-happy-life/.

Renken, Elena. "Most Americans Are Lonely, and Our Workplace Culture May Not Be Helping." *NPR.* January 23, 2020. https://www.npr.org/sections/health-shots/2020/01/23/798676465/most-americans-are-lonely-and-our-workplace-culture-may-not-be-helping.

Seppälä, Dr. Emma. "Connectedness & Health: The Science of Social Connection." *The Center for Compassion and Altruism Research and Education.* http://ccare.stanford.edu/uncategorized/connectedness-health-the-science-of-social-connection-infographic/.

Tate, Nick. "Loneliness Rivals Obesity, Smoking as Health Risk." *WebMD.* May 4, 2018. https://www.webmd.com/balance/news/20180504/loneliness-rivals-obesity-smoking-as-health-risk.

Wolpert, Stuart. "UCLA Neuroscientist's Book Explains Why Social Connection Is as Important as Food and Shelter." *UCLA Newsroom.* October 10, 2013. https://newsroom.ucla.edu/releases/we-are-hard-wired-to-be-social-248746.

Chapter 6: Inspire Confidence

Antanaityte, Neringa. "Mind Matters: How to Effortlessly Have More Positive Thoughts." *Mind Matters* (blog), *TLEX Institute.* Accessed March 1, 2021. https://tlexinstitute.com/how-to-effortlessly-have-more-positive-thoughts/.

Healthwise Staff. "Egocentric and Magical Thinking." *Healthwise*, May 27, 2020. https://www.uofmhealth.org/health-library/te6277.

Chapter 7: Strength Redefined

"Excerpt from Brené Brown's Rising Strong: The Physics of Vulnerability." *Parade*. September 4, 2015. https://parade.com/420360/parade/excerpt-from-brene-browns-rising-strong-the-physics-of-vulnerability/.

Stanton, Andrew, dir. *Finding Nemo*. 2003; Emeryville, CA: Pixar. 2013. DVD.

Chapter 8: Failing Is Good

Cherry, Kendra. "The Psychology of How People Learn." *Verywell Mind,* May 28, 2020. https://www.verywellmind.com/what-is-learning-2795332.

Economy, Peter. "Use the 40 Percent Rule to Break through Every Obstacle and Achieve the Impossible." *Inc. Magazine*, April 23, 2019. https://www.inc.com/peter-economy/use-40-percent-rule-to-achieve-impossible.html.

Gladstone, India. "Here's What the World's Most Successful People Think about Failure." *Gentleman's Journal*. Accessed March 1, 2021. https://www.thegentlemansjournal.com/heres-worlds-successful-people-think-failure/.

"'If You Don't Give up, You Still Have a Chance. Giving up Is the Greatest Failure,' Says Jack Ma Yun." *The Silicon Review*, May 31, 2018. https://thesiliconreview.com/2018/05/if-you-dont-give-up-you-still-have-a-chance-giving-up-is-the-greatest-failure-says-jack-ma-yun.

Schwanzes, Rachel. "Science Says 92 Percent of People Don't Achieve Their Goals. Here's How the Other 8 Percent Do." *Inc. Magazine*, July 26, 2016. https://www.inc.com/marcel-schwantes/science-says-92-percent-of-people-dont-achieve-goals-heres-how-the-other-8-perce.html.

Chapter 9: Work with Others, for Others

Covey, Stephen. *The 7 Habits of Highly Effective People: Powerful Lessons in Personal Change.* New York: Free Press, 2004.

Linnig, Ulrike. "Collaboration Is Hard!" *Climate-KIC.* May 24, 2019. https://www.climate-kic.org/opinion/collaboration-is-hard/.

"We Have Two Ears and One Mouth So That We Can Listen Twice as Much as We Speak." *Cornell University Urban Semester* (blog). *Cornell University.* October 19, 2011. https://blogs.cornell.edu/cuus/2011/10/19/we-have-two-ears-and-one-mouth-so-that-we-can-listen-twice-as-much-as-we-speak/.

Chapter 10: Listen with Your Heart

The 5 Love Languages. "Quizzes." Accessed March 1, 2021. https://www.5lovelanguages.com/quizzes/.

Chapter 11: Live Your Life Purposefully

Honarvar, Zack. "Yes Theory's Manager Zack Honarvar: Why Creators Need CEOs Not Managers, the Business Side of Yes Theory." Interview by Jacob Kelly. *My Social Life*, July 27, 2020. Audio, 1:40:51. https://www.jacobkelly.ca/zack-honarvar.

Kwik, Jim. "Jim Kwik - Creator Series." Interview by Eric Koester. Otter.ai, September 29, 2020. Audio, 38:42. https://otter.ai/u/RV-yMD4kFpzj14NNAst3lM-ELAM.

Pirie, Madsen. "Death and Taxes." November 13, 2019. https://www.adamsmith.org/blog/death-and-taxes.

TEDx Talks. "Start with Why -- How Great Leaders Inspire Action | Simon Sinek | TedxPugetSound." September 28, 2009. Video, 18:01. https://www.youtube.com/watch?v=u-4ZoJKF_VuA&vl=en.

Chapter 12: It's the Little Things

TED-Ed. "Everyday Leadership - Drew Dudley." August 15, 2003. Video, 6:14. https://www.youtube.com/watch?v=uA-y6EawKKME.

Chapter 13: Learn How to Juggle

Bologna, Caroline. "8 Times Jada Pinkett Smith Totally Nailed the Whole Parenting Thing." *HuffPost.* September 18, 2017. https://www.huffpost.com/entry/8-times-jada-pinkett-smith-totally-nailed-the-whole-parenting-thing_n_59ba16eae4b02da0e13f2fdb.

EISENHOWER. "The Eisenhower Matrix: How to Manage Your Tasks with Eisenhower." September 2, 2012. Video, 2:24. https://www.youtube.com/watch?v=tT89OZ7TNwc&feature=emb_logo.

Honarvar, Zack. "Yes Theory's Manager Zack Honarvar: Why Creators Need CEOs Not Managers, the Business Side of Yes Theory." Interview by Jacob Kelly. *My Social Life*, July 27, 2020. Audio, 1:40:51. https://www.jacobkelly.ca/zack-honarvar.

Mel Robbins. "How to Stop Feeling Overwhelmed Right Now | Mel Robbins." August 13, 2018. Video, 3:42. https://www.youtube.com/watch?v=4zEBjqhwobA.

Mendelsohn, Pamela. "The Importance of Saying 'No.'" *MyTherapyNYC*. July 26, 2019. https://mytherapynyc.com/importance-of-saying-no/.

Chapter 14: Lead Yourself

Gebilagin, Lizza. "Reach Your Potential: Life Lessons from John Maclean Who Learned to Walk Again." *The Daily Telegraph,* January 15, 2017. https://www.dailytelegraph.com.au/lifestyle/health/body-soul-daily/reach-your-potential-life-lessons-from-john-maclean-who-learned-to-walk-again/news-story/1076def92fd52a7648ba50213733077c.

Meier, J.D. "The Best Stephen Covey Quotes That Will Empower You." *Sources of Insight*. https://sourcesofinsight.com/stephen-covey-quotes/.

Chapter 15: Reminders

Robinson, Elizabeth. "Storytelling versus Storymaking." *Max Influence* (blog). *MtoM Consulting*, November 17, 2014. https://mtomconsulting.com/storytelling-versus-storymaking/.

Made in the USA
Middletown, DE
10 May 2021

39352820R00116